HOW IT WORKS

DISCOVERING
PREHISTORY

Robert Muir Wood

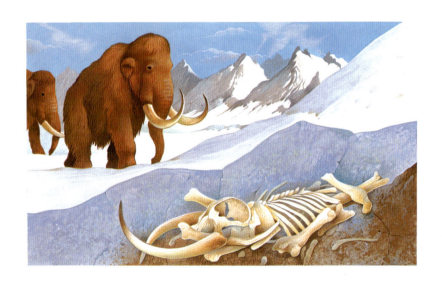

HORUS EDITIONS

ISBN 1-899762-38-8

Copyright © 1996 Horus Editions Limited

First published 1996
This edition first published 1997
Fourth impression 2000

Published by Horus Editions Limited,
1st floor, 27 Longford Street,
London NW1 3DZ

Printed in Singapore

HOW IT WORKS

CONTENTS

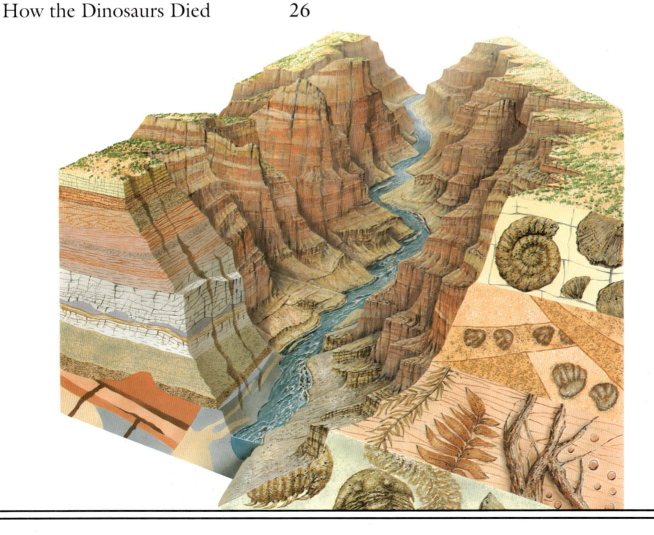

What is Prehistory?

HOW OLD is the Earth?
Have the continents moved?
How are mountains formed?
How do we know about the
dinosaurs? Where did people come from?
Such questions can only be answered by
exploring prehistory.

Prehistory means before history – that
is, before our earliest written records, which
go back about 4,000 years. Prehistory
covers a much longer period – the billions
of years of deep time. To explore prehistory
we need all the skills of a detective,
searching for clues preserved in the Earth.

THE FIRST BIRDS, SUCH AS
ARCHAEOPTERYX, EVOLVED
FROM THE REPTILES

IN THE TERTIARY PERIOD,
MAMMALS GREW TO BECOME
THE LARGEST ANIMALS ON
BOTH LAND AND SEA

THIS EARLY MAMMAL
EVOLVED INTO THE HORSE

WE LIVE AT THE END OF
THE QUATERNARY PERIOD

WOOLLY MAMMOTHS LIVED
IN THE QUATERNARY ICE AGES

PEOPLE EVOLVED AT THE
END OF THE TERTIARY
PERIOD, ABOUT 3 MILLION
YEARS AGO

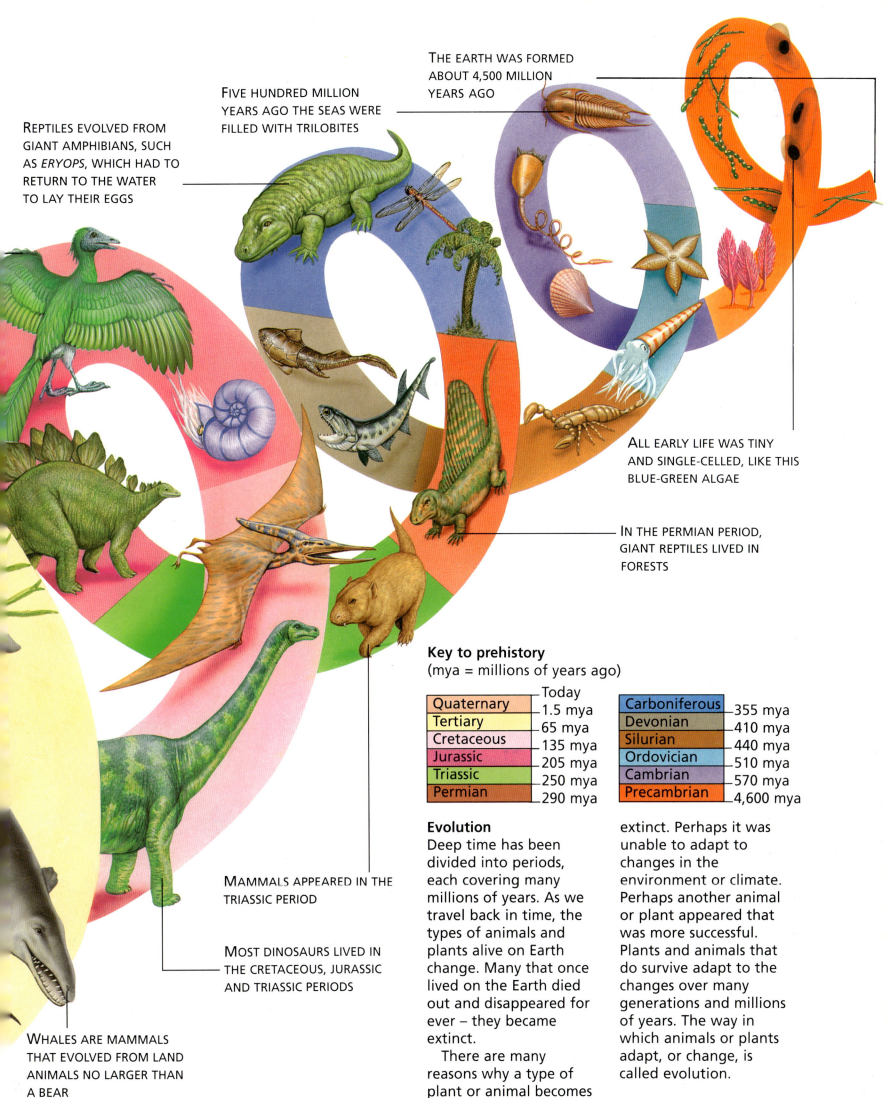

THE EARTH WAS FORMED ABOUT 4,500 MILLION YEARS AGO

FIVE HUNDRED MILLION YEARS AGO THE SEAS WERE FILLED WITH TRILOBITES

REPTILES EVOLVED FROM GIANT AMPHIBIANS, SUCH AS *ERYOPS*, WHICH HAD TO RETURN TO THE WATER TO LAY THEIR EGGS

ALL EARLY LIFE WAS TINY AND SINGLE-CELLED, LIKE THIS BLUE-GREEN ALGAE

IN THE PERMIAN PERIOD, GIANT REPTILES LIVED IN FORESTS

MAMMALS APPEARED IN THE TRIASSIC PERIOD

MOST DINOSAURS LIVED IN THE CRETACEOUS, JURASSIC AND TRIASSIC PERIODS

WHALES ARE MAMMALS THAT EVOLVED FROM LAND ANIMALS NO LARGER THAN A BEAR

Key to prehistory
(mya = millions of years ago)

Quaternary	Today
	1.5 mya
Tertiary	65 mya
Cretaceous	135 mya
Jurassic	205 mya
Triassic	250 mya
Permian	290 mya

Carboniferous	355 mya
Devonian	410 mya
Silurian	440 mya
Ordovician	510 mya
Cambrian	570 mya
Precambrian	4,600 mya

Evolution

Deep time has been divided into periods, each covering many millions of years. As we travel back in time, the types of animals and plants alive on Earth change. Many that once lived on the Earth died out and disappeared for ever – they became extinct.

There are many reasons why a type of plant or animal becomes extinct. Perhaps it was unable to adapt to changes in the environment or climate. Perhaps another animal or plant appeared that was more successful. Plants and animals that do survive adapt to the changes over many generations and millions of years. The way in which animals or plants adapt, or change, is called evolution.

Digging Up the Past

TO UNCOVER the past we have to dig down into the Earth. Sometimes rivers have done much of the work, by cutting gorges into the land. In Arizona, USA, the Colorado River has cut a gorge down through more than a kilometre of rock. This gorge, called the Grand Canyon, shows a spectacular section of the prehistoric past. Walking to the bottom of the Canyon, you can almost walk back in time: the layers of rock around you, and the fossils found within them, get older the further down you go.

SEDIMENTS FORMED OVER THE PAST 250 MILLION YEARS HAVE BEEN WORN AWAY

A SIMPLE RULE OF SEDIMENTS: YOUNGER LAYERS ARE FOUND ON TOP OF OLDER ONES

KAIBAB LIMESTONE (250 MILLION YEARS OLD)

COCONINO SANDSTONE (290 MILLION YEARS OLD)

HERMIT SHALE (350 MILLION YEARS OLD)

FOSSILS OF FISH SCALES ARE FOUND IN THIS LAYER, WHICH IS 390 MILLION YEARS OLD

BRIGHT ANGEL SHALE (530 MILLION YEARS OLD)

THE ROCKS HERE ARE MUCH OLDER AND HAVE TILTED DURING THE FORMATION OF MOUNTAINS

MOUNTAINS ARE WORN AWAY

RIVER SEDIMENT

LAKE SEDIMENT

DEEP-SEA SEDIMENT

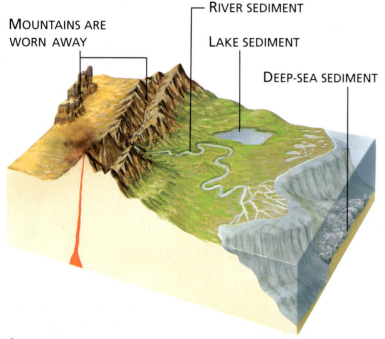

How the layers formed

Mountains are continually worn away. Fragments of the mountain are carried off by ice, water and wind, finally settling on lowland, or beneath the water of a lake or sea. These deposits are called sediments. Over millions of years layers of sediment pile up and harden, forming sedimentary rocks.

THESE ROCKS FORMED 1,700 MILLION YEARS AGO, WHEN THE ONLY LIFE ON EARTH WAS TINY SINGLE-CELLED ORGANISMS

THE RIVER CUTS DOWN THROUGH THE CANYON ROCKS

Fossils in layers
The age of a layer of sediments is known from the fossils found within it (*see pages 10–11*). Fossils are the remains of living things preserved in rock. As a result of evolution, life has changed through time. Fossils show us the different life forms that have lived during each period of prehistory. Here, some of the layers that contain fossils are shown enlarged.

Kaibab limestone (1)
Near the top of the Grand Canyon is a layer of Kaibab limestone and sandstone. This was deposited in a shallow sea 250 million years ago and is filled with the fossil shells of sea-living creatures such as ammonites.

Coconino sandstone (2)
The Coconino sandstone sediment was laid down on land about 290 million years ago. It contains footprints of primitive reptiles and amphibians, which lived before the dinosaurs.

Hermit shale (3)
Below the sandstone is Hermit shale. Laid down around 350 million years ago in shallow pools, these mudstones contain raindrop prints, and fossils of insects and ferns.

Bright Angel shale (4)
This shale was deposited when there were no plants or animals on land. Fossils include trilobites (ancient sea creatures), shells and creatures' burrow marks, of 530 million years ago.

9

How Fossils Form

FOSSILS have taught us most of what we know about prehistoric plants and animals. They are the traces of past life preserved in rock. Most are formed from the hard parts of animals and plants, but fossils can also record marks such as an animal's footprint left in sand. In order for something to become fossilized it must be buried in sediments quickly before it starts to decay away. As new layers of sediments are deposited on top, the lower layers become squashed, or compressed, into rock. In this way the animal or plant fragment in the lower layers becomes fossilized.

ONLY WHEN AN ANIMAL IS SUDDENLY COVERED IN SEDIMENT, PERHAPS IN A VOLCANIC ERUPTION, WILL ITS BONES STAY TOGETHER

DELICATE PLANT MATERIAL ONLY STAYS IN ONE PIECE IF IT IS COVERED WITH MUD OR STAGNANT WATER

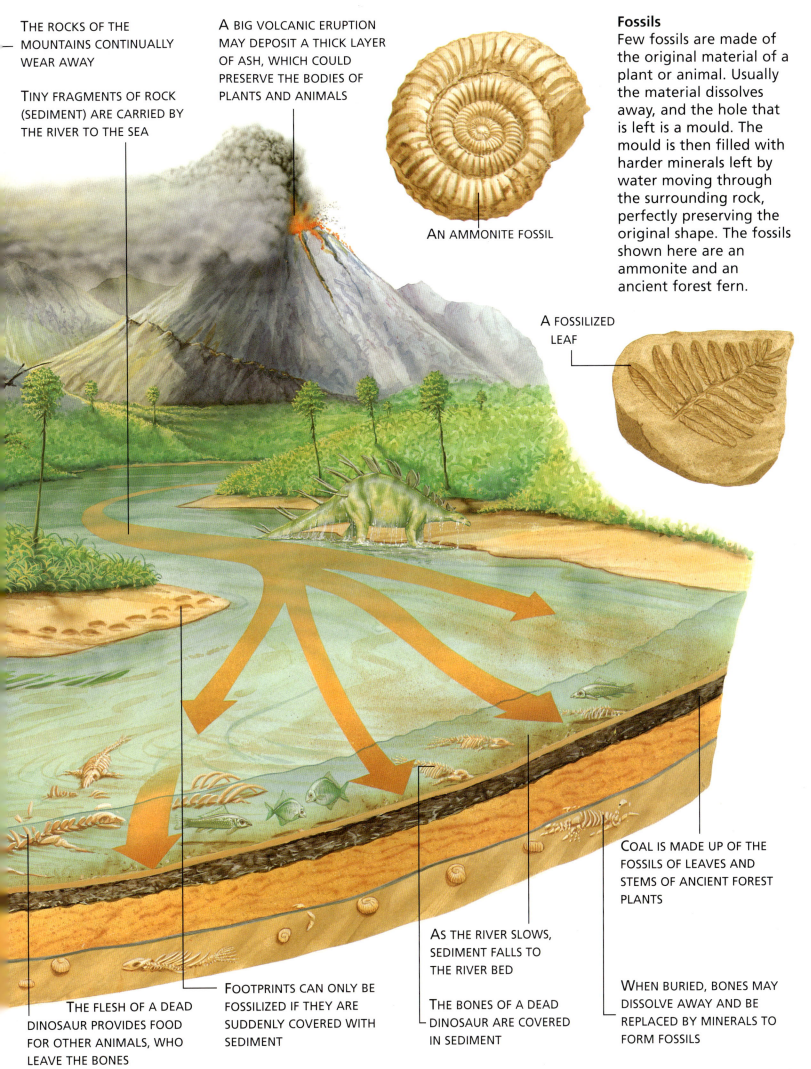

THE ROCKS OF THE MOUNTAINS CONTINUALLY WEAR AWAY

TINY FRAGMENTS OF ROCK (SEDIMENT) ARE CARRIED BY THE RIVER TO THE SEA

A BIG VOLCANIC ERUPTION MAY DEPOSIT A THICK LAYER OF ASH, WHICH COULD PRESERVE THE BODIES OF PLANTS AND ANIMALS

AN AMMONITE FOSSIL

Fossils
Few fossils are made of the original material of a plant or animal. Usually the material dissolves away, and the hole that is left is a mould. The mould is then filled with harder minerals left by water moving through the surrounding rock, perfectly preserving the original shape. The fossils shown here are an ammonite and an ancient forest fern.

A FOSSILIZED LEAF

THE FLESH OF A DEAD DINOSAUR PROVIDES FOOD FOR OTHER ANIMALS, WHO LEAVE THE BONES

FOOTPRINTS CAN ONLY BE FOSSILIZED IF THEY ARE SUDDENLY COVERED WITH SEDIMENT

AS THE RIVER SLOWS, SEDIMENT FALLS TO THE RIVER BED

THE BONES OF A DEAD DINOSAUR ARE COVERED IN SEDIMENT

COAL IS MADE UP OF THE FOSSILS OF LEAVES AND STEMS OF ANCIENT FOREST PLANTS

WHEN BURIED, BONES MAY DISSOLVE AWAY AND BE REPLACED BY MINERALS TO FORM FOSSILS

11

Comparing Evidence

NO SINGLE place on Earth can give us a complete record of prehistory. Parts of the record are found scattered in different areas of the world. To link these fragments together we have to find materials that were formed in different places but at the same time. This process is called correlation. We can also date layers in the soil by correlating objects made by people. For example, we know that bronze was not used by people until about 5,000 years ago. So wherever a bronze item is found, we know the soil it was found in is not more than 5,000 years old.

Tools and treasures
One form of correlation uses the objects made by early peoples. The first tools and arrowheads, made from flint and other stone (1), were made to a similar design for tens of thousands of years. The first carved figures date from more than 20,000 years ago (2). By 10,000 BC people started to bake pottery jars and cups. They travelled thousands of kilometres and exchanged their new ideas with other peoples. The discovery of how to make bronze, around 3000 BC, led to new ornaments being made (3). And with the discovery of iron-smelting around 1000 BC, new, more effective weapons were possible (4). So, when we find an iron weapon we know it must date from after 1000 BC.

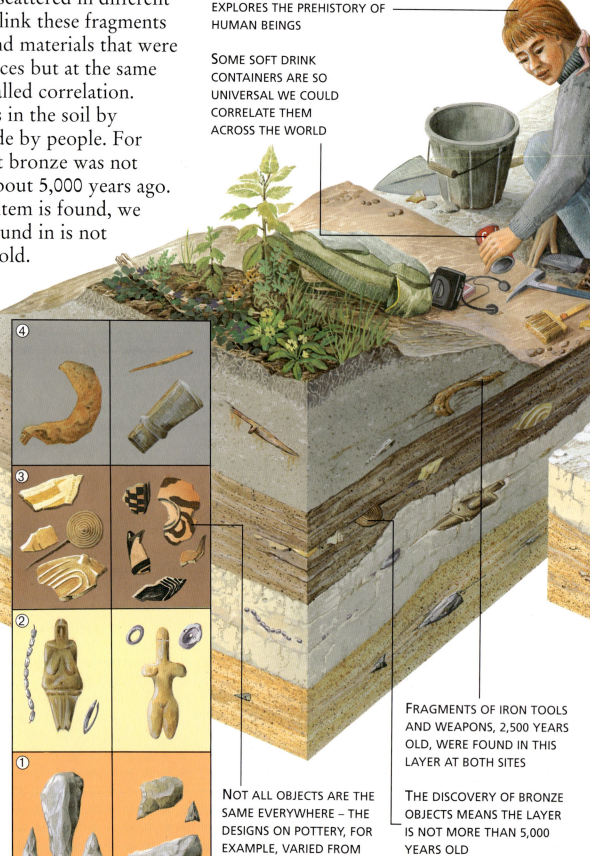

AN ARCHAEOLOGIST EXPLORES THE PREHISTORY OF HUMAN BEINGS

SOME SOFT DRINK CONTAINERS ARE SO UNIVERSAL WE COULD CORRELATE THEM ACROSS THE WORLD

④ ③ ② ①

NOT ALL OBJECTS ARE THE SAME EVERYWHERE – THE DESIGNS ON POTTERY, FOR EXAMPLE, VARIED FROM REGION TO REGION

FRAGMENTS OF IRON TOOLS AND WEAPONS, 2,500 YEARS OLD, WERE FOUND IN THIS LAYER AT BOTH SITES

THE DISCOVERY OF BRONZE OBJECTS MEANS THE LAYER IS NOT MORE THAN 5,000 YEARS OLD

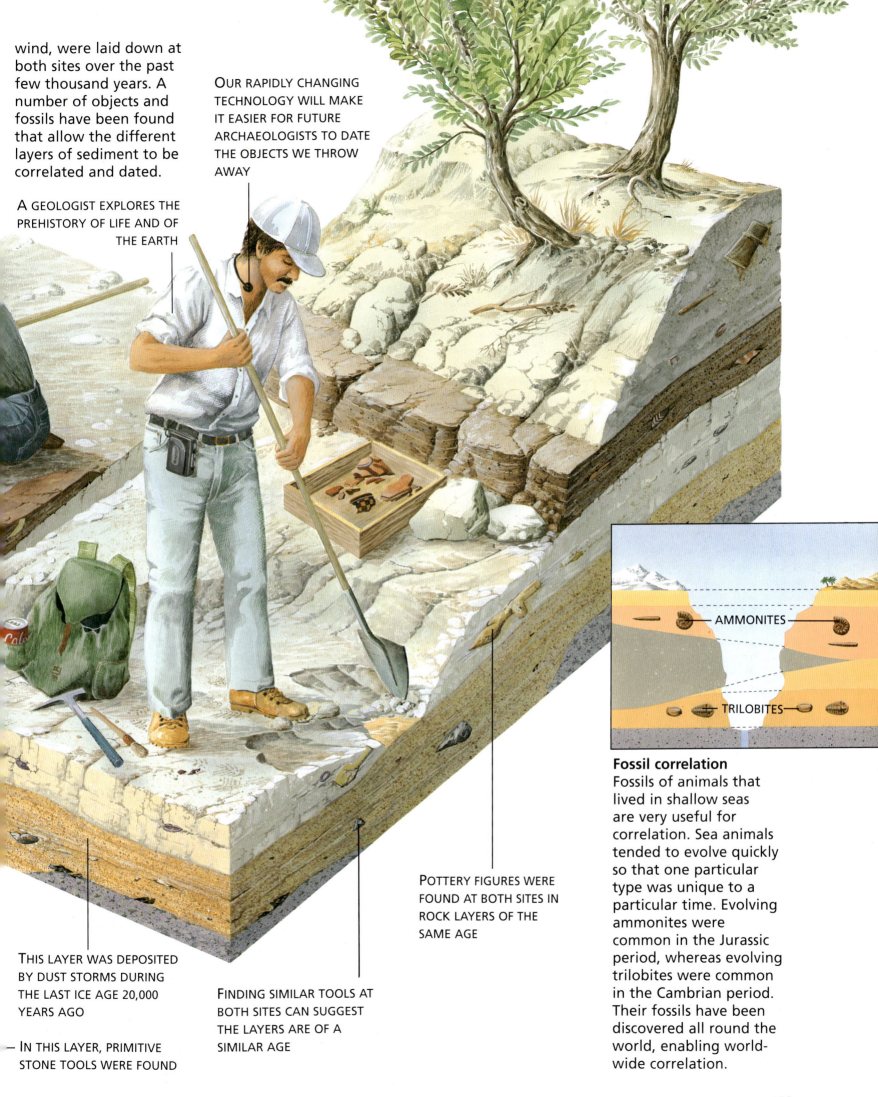

wind, were laid down at both sites over the past few thousand years. A number of objects and fossils have been found that allow the different layers of sediment to be correlated and dated.

OUR RAPIDLY CHANGING TECHNOLOGY WILL MAKE IT EASIER FOR FUTURE ARCHAEOLOGISTS TO DATE THE OBJECTS WE THROW AWAY

A GEOLOGIST EXPLORES THE PREHISTORY OF LIFE AND OF THE EARTH

AMMONITES

TRILOBITES

Fossil correlation
Fossils of animals that lived in shallow seas are very useful for correlation. Sea animals tended to evolve quickly so that one particular type was unique to a particular time. Evolving ammonites were common in the Jurassic period, whereas evolving trilobites were common in the Cambrian period. Their fossils have been discovered all round the world, enabling world-wide correlation.

POTTERY FIGURES WERE FOUND AT BOTH SITES IN ROCK LAYERS OF THE SAME AGE

THIS LAYER WAS DEPOSITED BY DUST STORMS DURING THE LAST ICE AGE 20,000 YEARS AGO

IN THIS LAYER, PRIMITIVE STONE TOOLS WERE FOUND

FINDING SIMILAR TOOLS AT BOTH SITES CAN SUGGEST THE LAYERS ARE OF A SIMILAR AGE

Continuous Cores

SOME parts of nature hold secrets of their age within them. In the same way that we can follow the evolution of the Earth by digging into it, we can study the passing of time by looking at the layers in the wood of a tree or the ice of an ice-sheet. Taking out a core from a tree or an ice-sheet allows us to count the years back into the past. Such cores record changes in the pattern of the weather, some of which can be correlated around the globe.

Tree cores

Trees do most of their growing in the summer. If a tree trunk is cut across its width, you can see a pattern of rings: wider bands of spring early-wood, separated by narrow, darker bands of autumn and winter late-wood. Changes in climate alter the widths of the rings from year to year. By studying the ring patterns and matching them against older tree cores, we can learn how the climate has changed over thousands of years.

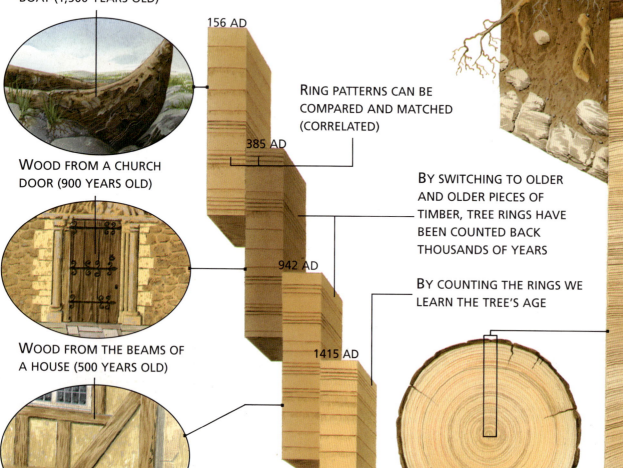

USING A NARROW CORER, IT IS POSSIBLE TO OBTAIN A CONTINUOUS SECTION THROUGH A LIVING TREE WITHOUT DAMAGING IT

A CORE TAKEN FROM THE CENTRE OF A LIVING TREE

WOOD FROM A PREHISTORIC BOAT (1,500 YEARS OLD)

WOOD FROM A CHURCH DOOR (900 YEARS OLD)

WOOD FROM THE BEAMS OF A HOUSE (500 YEARS OLD)

156 AD

385 AD

942 AD

1415 AD

RING PATTERNS CAN BE COMPARED AND MATCHED (CORRELATED)

BY SWITCHING TO OLDER AND OLDER PIECES OF TIMBER, TREE RINGS HAVE BEEN COUNTED BACK THOUSANDS OF YEARS

BY COUNTING THE RINGS WE LEARN THE TREE'S AGE

THICK RINGS REVEAL LONG, WARM, WET SUMMERS

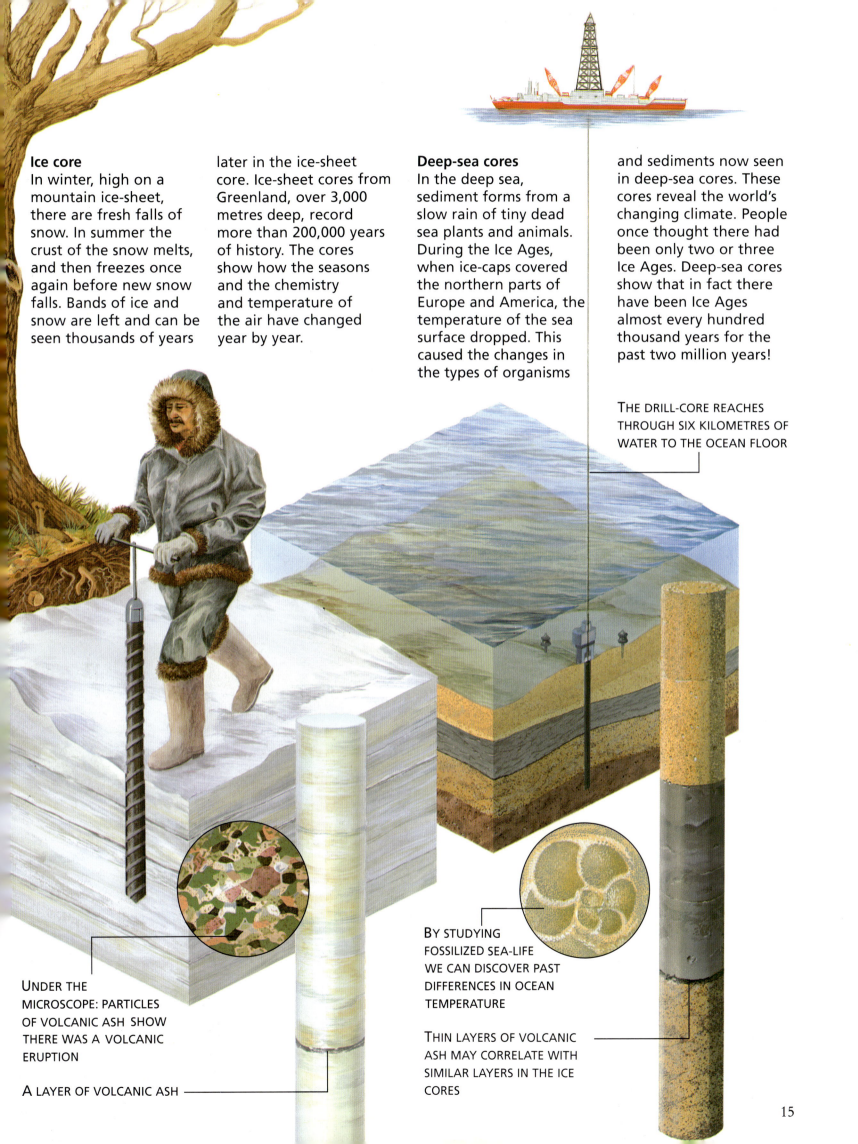

Ice core

In winter, high on a mountain ice-sheet, there are fresh falls of snow. In summer the crust of the snow melts, and then freezes once again before new snow falls. Bands of ice and snow are left and can be seen thousands of years later in the ice-sheet core. Ice-sheet cores from Greenland, over 3,000 metres deep, record more than 200,000 years of history. The cores show how the seasons and the chemistry and temperature of the air have changed year by year.

Deep-sea cores

In the deep sea, sediment forms from a slow rain of tiny dead sea plants and animals. During the Ice Ages, when ice-caps covered the northern parts of Europe and America, the temperature of the sea surface dropped. This caused the changes in the types of organisms and sediments now seen in deep-sea cores. These cores reveal the world's changing climate. People once thought there had been only two or three Ice Ages. Deep-sea cores show that in fact there have been Ice Ages almost every hundred thousand years for the past two million years!

THE DRILL-CORE REACHES THROUGH SIX KILOMETRES OF WATER TO THE OCEAN FLOOR

UNDER THE MICROSCOPE: PARTICLES OF VOLCANIC ASH SHOW THERE WAS A VOLCANIC ERUPTION

A LAYER OF VOLCANIC ASH

BY STUDYING FOSSILIZED SEA-LIFE WE CAN DISCOVER PAST DIFFERENCES IN OCEAN TEMPERATURE

THIN LAYERS OF VOLCANIC ASH MAY CORRELATE WITH SIMILAR LAYERS IN THE ICE CORES

Counting Radio-isotopes

THE YEARS of deep time can be charted in rocks. Rocks contain radio-isotopes – atoms that are unstable and fall apart (decay) at a constant rate. A large number of these radio-isotope atoms slowly change from parent atoms to daughter atoms. The age of a rock can be found by measuring how many of the parent atoms have decayed into daughter atoms. For some radio-isotopes millions of years will pass before they have all become daughter atoms.

The radio-isotope of the element potassium is useful for dating prehistory because it is found in many ancient rocks. The parent atom potassium decays into the daughter atom argon. By counting the radio-isotopes we can find the age of ancient rocks that are sometimes billions of years old. Radio-isotope dating provides a calendar of prehistory, helping us to reconstruct the past.

Volcanic rocks (1)
Volcanic rocks, or lava, often contain potassium-rich minerals. By counting the radio-isotopes we can date when the volcano erupted. This could help us date the fossils of dinosaurs that died in the red-hot lava.

①

DATING THIS ROCK SHOWS THE VOLCANO ERUPTED 250 MILLION YEARS AGO

ONLY ONE POTASSIUM ATOM HAS BECOME AN ARGON ATOM

METEORITE CRATER

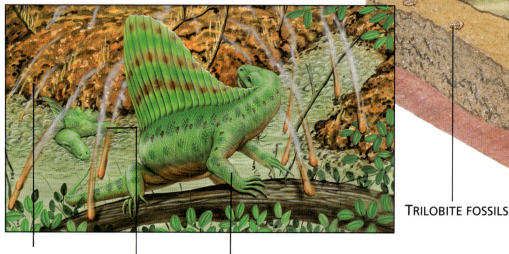

LAVA (MOLTEN ROCK FROM THE VOLCANO) RUNS ACROSS THE LAND

LAVA COOLS AND SOLIDIFIES OVER DINOSAUR REMAINS

FOSSILS SHOW THAT THE DINOSAUR *DIMETRODON* DIED IN THE ERUPTION

TRILOBITE FOSSILS

A LAYER OF SEDIMENTARY ROCK

ROCKS FROM THIS PREHISTORIC SCENE COULD BE FOUND TODAY, AND DATED

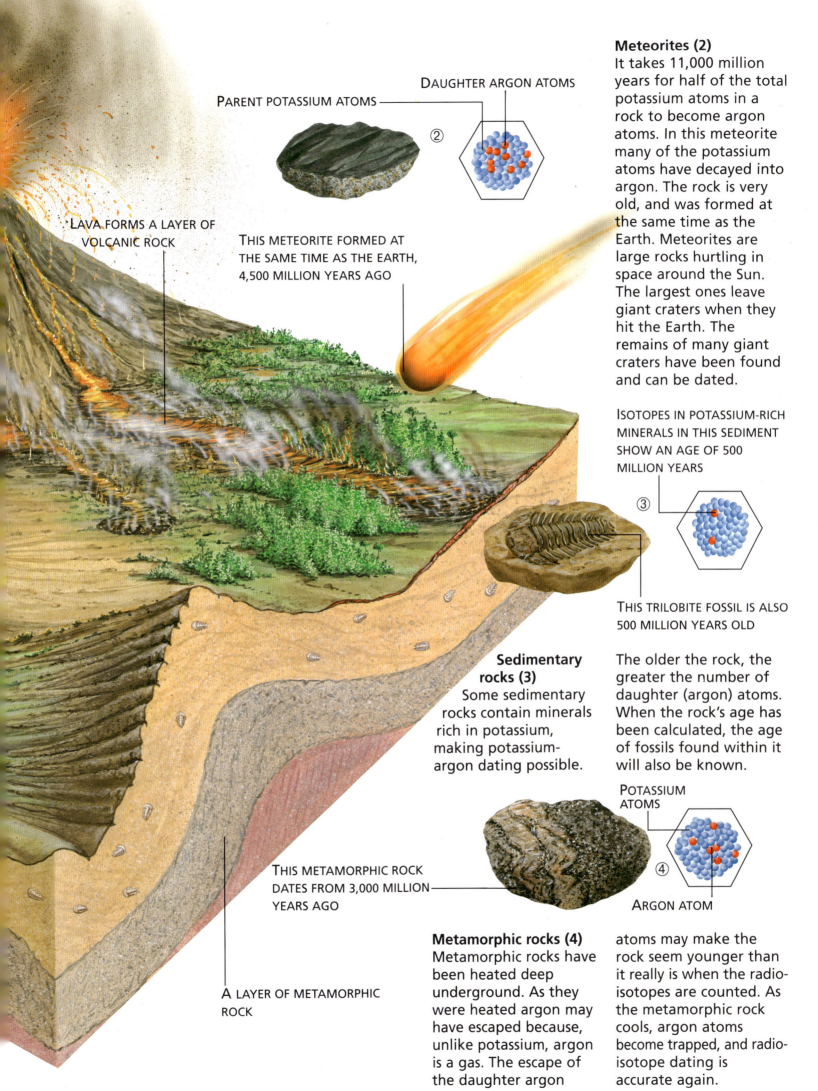

PARENT POTASSIUM ATOMS

DAUGHTER ARGON ATOMS

②

LAVA FORMS A LAYER OF VOLCANIC ROCK

THIS METEORITE FORMED AT THE SAME TIME AS THE EARTH, 4,500 MILLION YEARS AGO

Meteorites (2)

It takes 11,000 million years for half of the total potassium atoms in a rock to become argon atoms. In this meteorite many of the potassium atoms have decayed into argon. The rock is very old, and was formed at the same time as the Earth. Meteorites are large rocks hurtling in space around the Sun. The largest ones leave giant craters when they hit the Earth. The remains of many giant craters have been found and can be dated.

ISOTOPES IN POTASSIUM-RICH MINERALS IN THIS SEDIMENT SHOW AN AGE OF 500 MILLION YEARS

③

THIS TRILOBITE FOSSIL IS ALSO 500 MILLION YEARS OLD

Sedimentary rocks (3)

Some sedimentary rocks contain minerals rich in potassium, making potassium-argon dating possible.

The older the rock, the greater the number of daughter (argon) atoms. When the rock's age has been calculated, the age of fossils found within it will also be known.

POTASSIUM ATOMS

④

ARGON ATOM

THIS METAMORPHIC ROCK DATES FROM 3,000 MILLION YEARS AGO

A LAYER OF METAMORPHIC ROCK

Metamorphic rocks (4)

Metamorphic rocks have been heated deep underground. As they were heated argon may have escaped because, unlike potassium, argon is a gas. The escape of the daughter argon

atoms may make the rock seem younger than it really is when the radio-isotopes are counted. As the metamorphic rock cools, argon atoms become trapped, and radio-isotope dating is accurate again.

17

Radiocarbon Dating

RADIOCARBON (or carbon 14) dating gives archaeologists an accurate age of any formerly living material. While radio-isotope dating can be used for measuring rocks that have been around since the origin of the Earth, radiocarbon dating can only be used for dating material from the past 40,000 years.

Carbon 14 is a radioactive form of the element carbon that is continually being created at the top of the atmosphere. Carbon is taken up by plants. Animals (including humans) take in carbon 14 when they eat plants and when they breathe. When the plant or animal dies, carbon 14 is no longer taken in. But the carbon 14 left in the dead material gradually decays. By measuring the amount left in the material, archaeologists can tell how long it is since the organism died.

2,500 YEARS AGO

2,000 YEARS AGO

Carbon 14
When a tree is cut down, it dies and stops taking in more carbon 14 from the atmosphere. The tree might be made into a boat but the carbon 14 in the wood would continue to decay. After 5,730 years half the carbon 14 will have gone. After 11,460 years only a quarter will be left. Pictured left is a boat that was made by prehistoric farmers. Buried in the soil it gradually decayed. Radiocarbon dating of a piece of the boat today might show it as being 2,500 years old, with more than a quarter of the carbon 14 gone.

PLANTS ABSORB CARBON 14 IN CARBON DIOXIDE

Prehistoric farmers
This scene of prehistoric farmers shows how carbon 14 is taken in by the living plants and people of the time. If we found any dead remains from this prehistoric scene today, we would be able to date it using radiocarbon dating.

THE RADIOCARBON DATE OF THIS BOAT WOULD SHOW WHEN THE TREE DIED

REMAINS OF ALL THE LIVING OBJECTS IN THIS SCENE COULD BE RADIOCARBON DATED

CLOTH WOVEN FROM PLANTS, SUCH AS FLAX, CAN BE DATED

BY DATING THE REMAINS PRESERVED IN A BOG WE CAN RECONSTRUCT A SCENE LIKE THIS FROM 2,500 YEARS AGO

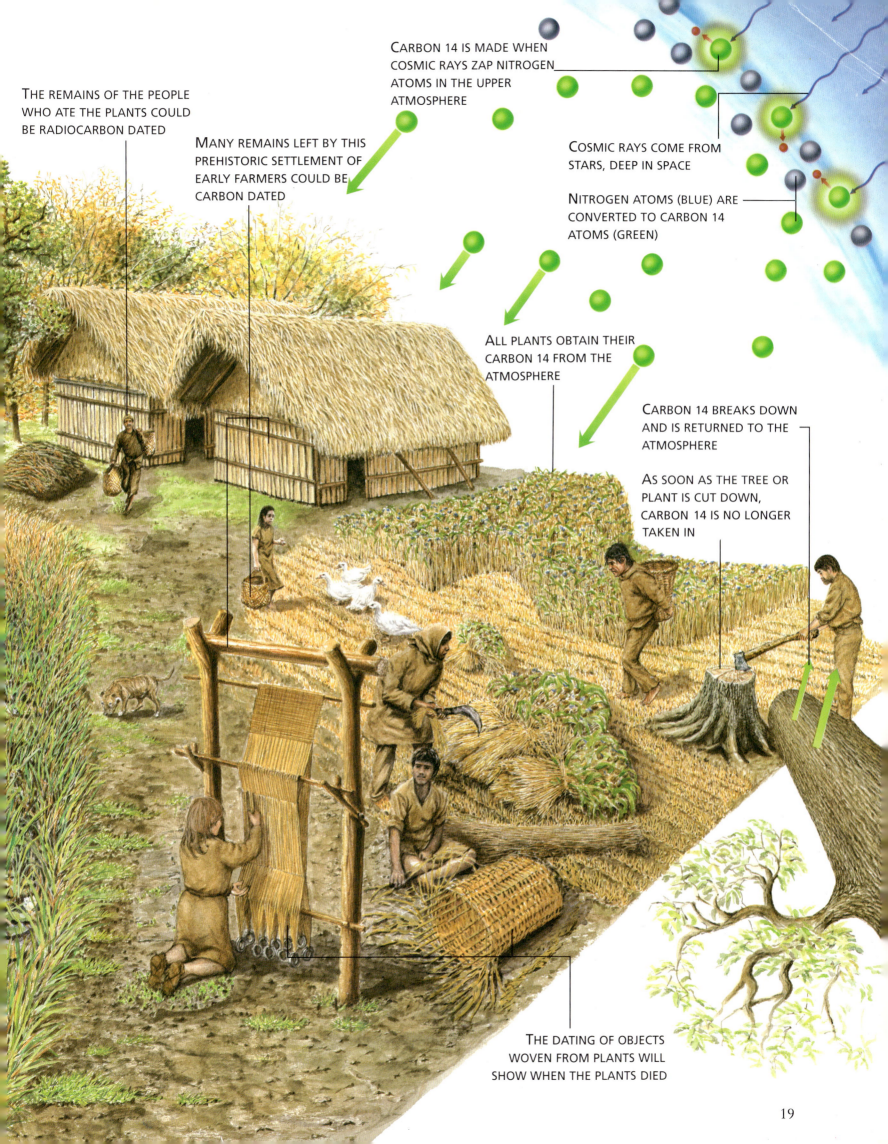

CARBON 14 IS MADE WHEN COSMIC RAYS ZAP NITROGEN ATOMS IN THE UPPER ATMOSPHERE

COSMIC RAYS COME FROM STARS, DEEP IN SPACE

NITROGEN ATOMS (BLUE) ARE CONVERTED TO CARBON 14 ATOMS (GREEN)

THE REMAINS OF THE PEOPLE WHO ATE THE PLANTS COULD BE RADIOCARBON DATED

MANY REMAINS LEFT BY THIS PREHISTORIC SETTLEMENT OF EARLY FARMERS COULD BE CARBON DATED

ALL PLANTS OBTAIN THEIR CARBON 14 FROM THE ATMOSPHERE

CARBON 14 BREAKS DOWN AND IS RETURNED TO THE ATMOSPHERE

AS SOON AS THE TREE OR PLANT IS CUT DOWN, CARBON 14 IS NO LONGER TAKEN IN

THE DATING OF OBJECTS WOVEN FROM PLANTS WILL SHOW WHEN THE PLANTS DIED

Dinosaur Excavation

IMPORTANT fossil finds require very careful digging or excavation. The first discovery may be the chance sighting of a fossil sticking out of a cliff or the glimpse of a bone as the foundations of a new building are being dug. This *Iguanodon* skeleton is unusually complete. The animal died and was preserved all in one place. Finds like this are very rare and demand the most careful excavation to ensure that nothing is broken and nothing is missed. To help rebuild the skeleton accurately, scientists have to record the location of every tiny fragment of bone.

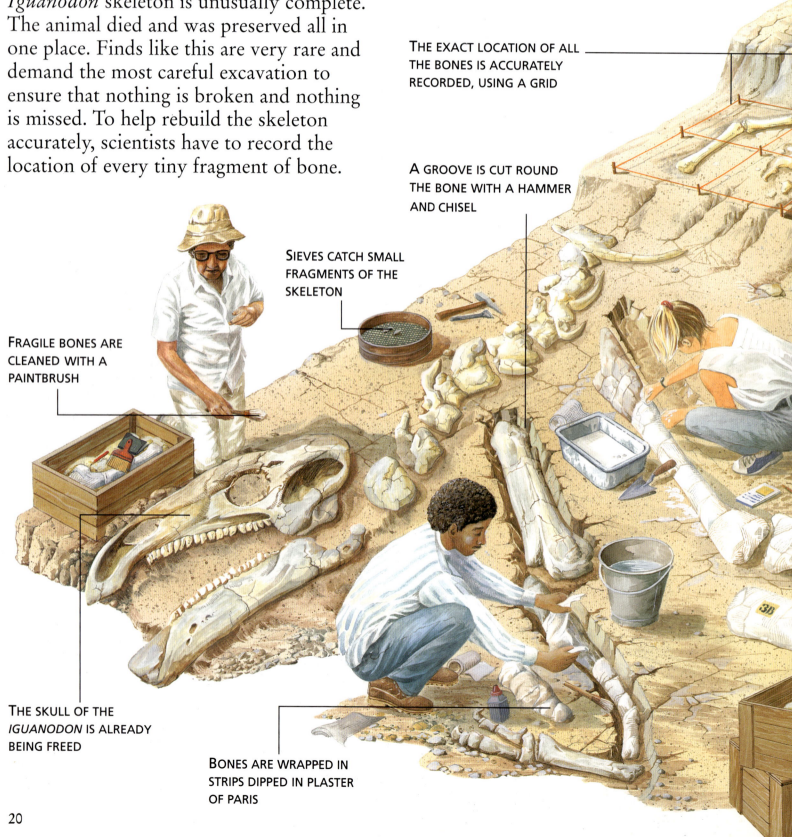

THE SITE IS EXCAVATED LAYER BY LAYER – A PICKAXE IS USED TO BREAK UP THE TOP LAYER OF ROCK

THE TOP LAYERS OF ROCK ARE REMOVED FIRST

THE EXACT LOCATION OF ALL THE BONES IS ACCURATELY RECORDED, USING A GRID

A GROOVE IS CUT ROUND THE BONE WITH A HAMMER AND CHISEL

SIEVES CATCH SMALL FRAGMENTS OF THE SKELETON

FRAGILE BONES ARE CLEANED WITH A PAINTBRUSH

THE SKULL OF THE *IGUANODON* IS ALREADY BEING FREED

BONES ARE WRAPPED IN STRIPS DIPPED IN PLASTER OF PARIS

In the laboratory

The jawbone is the strongest part of a skull and may be the only piece to survive. The amount the teeth are worn down can reveal the animal's age when it died, and the kind of food it ate.

The jawbone arrives in the laboratory in its protective covering. This is removed and any stone left on it is dissolved in weak acid.

Detailed cleaning is carried out using various tiny instruments, like a dentist's drill or a small chisel. The cleaned bone fragments are then carefully examined to see how they fitted together. The teeth can be put back into the jawbone and glued into place. Any missing pieces of bone or teeth are replaced with plaster. At this stage scientists can start to build up a picture of what the dinosaur was like.

EVERY FIND IS LISTED

THE PROTECTED BONES CAN BE GENTLY LIFTED AND PACKED IN CRATES

CRATES ARE WHEELED TO A LORRY, AND TAKEN TO THE LABORATORY

Dinosaur Reconstruction

WHAT did dinosaurs look like? The bones are impressive enough, but to flesh out the bones it is necessary to rebuild the whole dinosaur with muscles and skin. The first stage, putting a dinosaur skeleton together, is like solving a jigsaw puzzle. Some of the pieces may be missing and others badly broken. However, there are so many similarities between dinosaurs and animals living today, it is possible to find the right places for almost all the bones simply by comparing their shapes to those of today's animals. Once the skeleton has been formed, the muscles can be added, and then the skin.

THE MUSCLES HAD TO BE LARGE ENOUGH TO ALLOW *TRICERATOPS* TO CHARGE ITS ATTACKERS

THE MUSCLES OF DINOSAURS WERE SIMILAR IN SHAPE TO THOSE OF BIRDS AND CROCODILES

What is the skin like?
Fossilized fragments of dinosaur skin are sometimes found. The fragment above shows a pattern similar to that of a lizard's, but on a larger scale. The skin had to be very tough to withstand being dragged through spiny trees or bushes. Skin-colour does not show on the fossil.

TRICERATOPS WAS PROBABLY GREY, LIKE THE MODERN ANIMAL THAT SHARES A SIMILAR LIFESTYLE – THE RHINOCEROS

THE PATTERN OF MUSCLES CAN BE RECONSTRUCTED BY WORKING OUT HOW THE LIMBS MOVED

THE OVERALL SHAPE OF THE SKELETON SHOWS THAT IT WALKED ON ITS TOES

Where were the muscles attached?

There are often markings on the bones where large muscles were attached. From these muscle-scar markings, it is possible to begin to reconstruct the muscles of the legs and body.

HORNS WERE USED AS WEAPONS AGAINST ATTACK

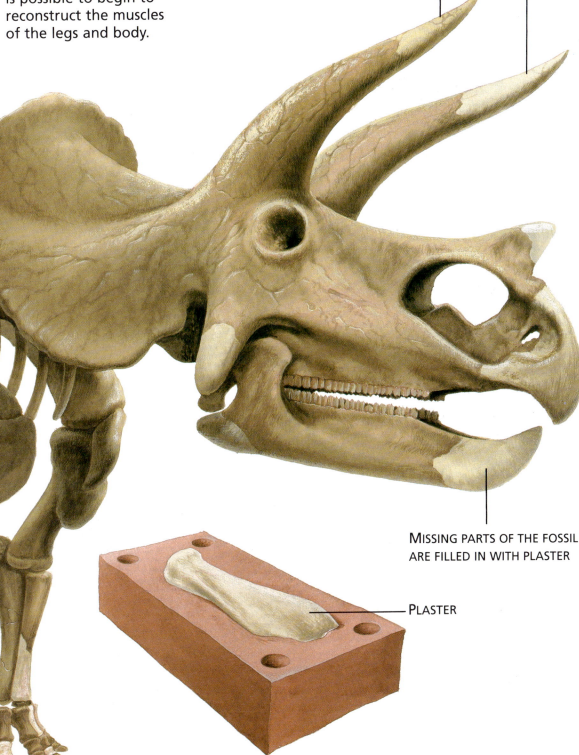

MISSING PARTS OF THE FOSSIL ARE FILLED IN WITH PLASTER

PLASTER

Missing bones

Many bones in a body are the same as other bones; one rib is very similar to another rib. If a bone is missing, either a copy can be made or it can be reconstructed from those that do exist. Cast in plaster, these newly made bones can be used to complete the skeleton.

Assembling the skeleton

First the whole skeleton is laid out on the floor (1).

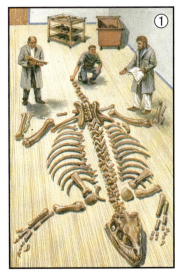

Starting with the spine, the vertebrae (back-bones) are wired together. The spine is then hauled into the air. The leg bones are put together and then attached to the spine (2).

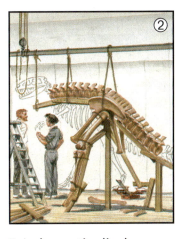

For dramatic displays, skeletons are assembled into life-like poses, such as a fighting scene, with their necks bent and jaws open (3). A metal frame is used to support the skeleton.

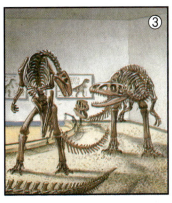

How the Dinosaurs Lived

WHAT were the dinosaurs like? Did they walk or run? How did they fight? What kind of noises did they make? Will we ever know how they lived? Just like any other animal, every part of a dinosaur's body helped it to survive. So every part of a dinosaur that we find tells us something about how it lived.

Several of the most amazing dinosaurs lived alongside each other. *Parasaurolophos* was a duck-billed dinosaur that lived in forests. The *Ankylosaur* was an armoured dinosaur that lived in open grassland. Both were attacked by the fearsome *Tyrannosaurus*. A few million years later these and all the other dinosaurs on Earth were dead.

Dinosaur nest
We know some dinosaurs had nesting colonies, where they laid their eggs together. The remains of some of these colonies have been found in fossilized form. These *Maiasaurus* nests were made of mounds of sand. Beside one nest there were fossils of 15 newly-hatched dinosaur babies.

A dinosaur's meal
We even know what a dinosaur last had to eat before it died. This *Compsognathus* had just eaten a lizard. The lizard's skeleton was fossilized in the dinosaur's ribcage.

THE FOSSIL OF A LIZARD'S SKELETON

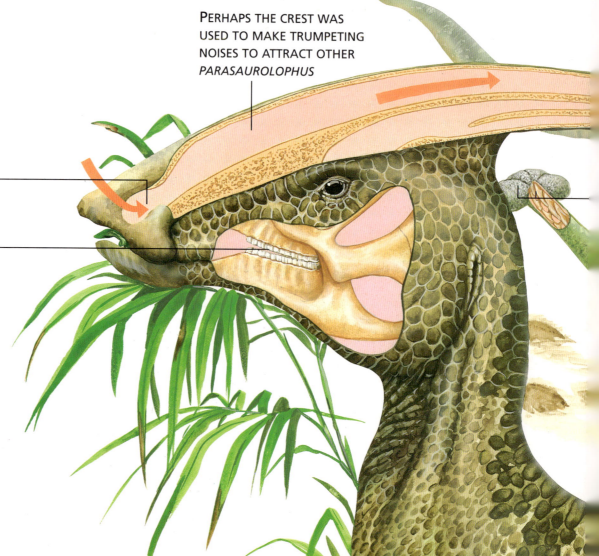

PERHAPS THE CREST WAS USED TO MAKE TRUMPETING NOISES TO ATTRACT OTHER *PARASAUROLOPHUS*

TUBES FOR AIR RAN THROUGH ITS CREST

THESE TEETH WERE SHAPED FOR GRINDING VEGETATION

A duck-billed dinosaur
This plant-eating *Parasaurolophos* is called a duck-billed dinosaur because of the crest on its head. The one-metre long crest was partly a colourful ornament to show off to other dinosaurs. But it also contained air tubes which may have given the animal an acute sense of smell.

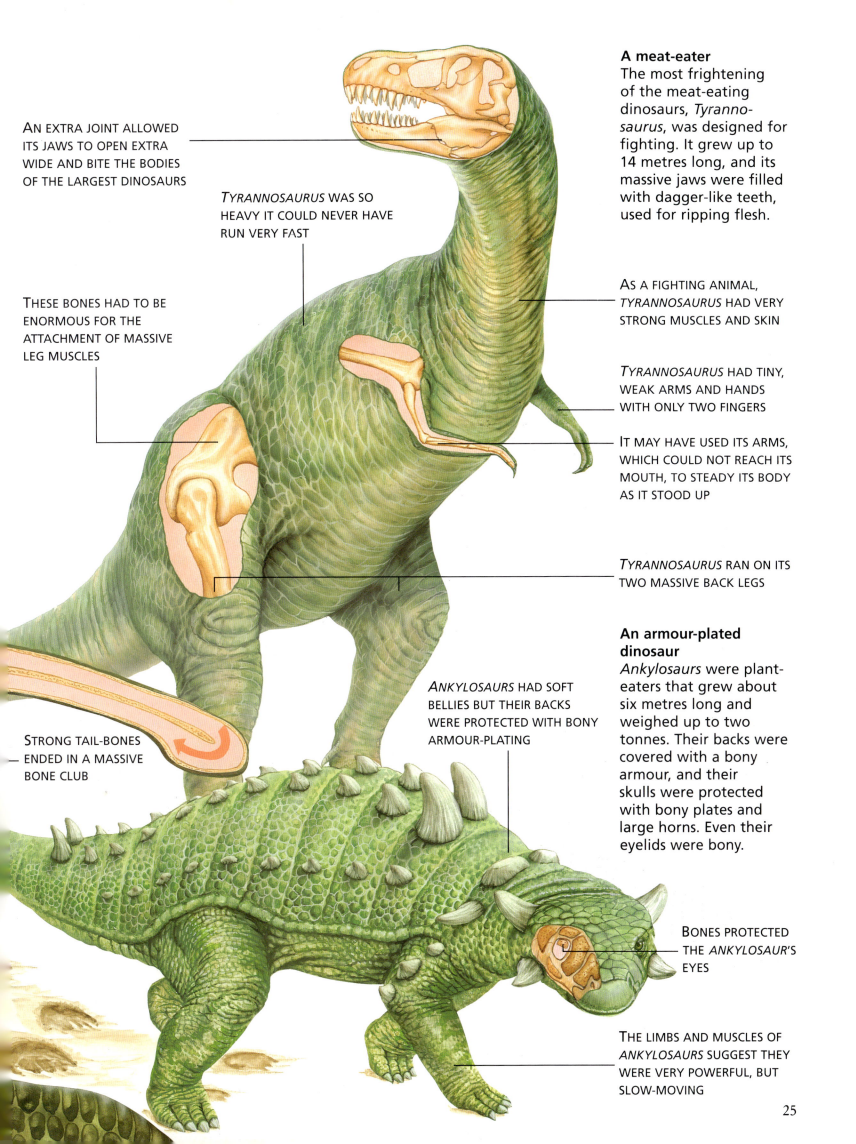

AN EXTRA JOINT ALLOWED ITS JAWS TO OPEN EXTRA WIDE AND BITE THE BODIES OF THE LARGEST DINOSAURS

A meat-eater
The most frightening of the meat-eating dinosaurs, *Tyrannosaurus*, was designed for fighting. It grew up to 14 metres long, and its massive jaws were filled with dagger-like teeth, used for ripping flesh.

TYRANNOSAURUS WAS SO HEAVY IT COULD NEVER HAVE RUN VERY FAST

THESE BONES HAD TO BE ENORMOUS FOR THE ATTACHMENT OF MASSIVE LEG MUSCLES

AS A FIGHTING ANIMAL, *TYRANNOSAURUS* HAD VERY STRONG MUSCLES AND SKIN

TYRANNOSAURUS HAD TINY, WEAK ARMS AND HANDS WITH ONLY TWO FINGERS

IT MAY HAVE USED ITS ARMS, WHICH COULD NOT REACH ITS MOUTH, TO STEADY ITS BODY AS IT STOOD UP

TYRANNOSAURUS RAN ON ITS TWO MASSIVE BACK LEGS

An armour-plated dinosaur
Ankylosaurs were plant-eaters that grew about six metres long and weighed up to two tonnes. Their backs were covered with a bony armour, and their skulls were protected with bony plates and large horns. Even their eyelids were bony.

ANKYLOSAURS HAD SOFT BELLIES BUT THEIR BACKS WERE PROTECTED WITH BONY ARMOUR-PLATING

STRONG TAIL-BONES ENDED IN A MASSIVE BONE CLUB

BONES PROTECTED THE *ANKYLOSAUR'S* EYES

THE LIMBS AND MUSCLES OF *ANKYLOSAURS* SUGGEST THEY WERE VERY POWERFUL, BUT SLOW-MOVING

How the Dinosaurs Died

DINOSAURS ruled the Earth for 150 million years. Then, quite suddenly, 65 million years ago, all the dinosaurs died. They were not, however, the only animals to become extinct at this time. Many animals living in the sea also disappeared along with many varieties of tiny sea-dwelling plants. The remains of these plants and animals settled on the sea and river beds. Over millions of years these remains formed layers of sedimentary rock. It is this rock which helps us understand why the dinosaurs disappeared. The main cause appears to have been an asteroid that collided with the Earth, causing massive damage. But sediments in the rock suggest other causes, too, such as volcanic activity and climate change.

AN ASTEROID IS A MOUNTAIN-SIZED BOULDER FROM OUTER SPACE

A DUST CLOUD MAY HAVE FILLED THE SKY

THE GIANT CRATER FORMED BY SUCH AN ASTEROID HAS BEEN FOUND BENEATH THE COAST OF MEXICO

PERHAPS THE EARTH BECAME POISONED BY CLOUDS OF VOLCANIC GAS AND DUST

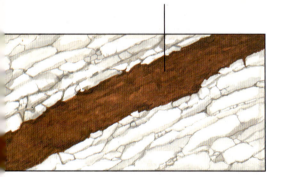

A DARK LAYER FORMED WHEN SEA-LIFE HAD ALMOST DISAPPEARED

Death in the sea
Climate also changed at this time. A drop in temperature, as a result of thick smoke and dust in the air, would explain why so many animals died. In many parts of the world, amidst thick layers of chalk (formed from the remains of sea-life) a dark layer of clay records where life almost ended.

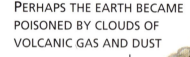

A LAYER RICH IN CHARCOAL

Forest fires
Tiny particles of burnt wood, or charcoal, have been found in sediments laid down at the time the dinosaurs died. This charcoal must have come from huge forest fires, perhaps covering millions of square kilometres. Many of the dinosaurs may have perished in the fires and smoke.

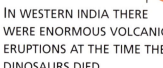

IN WESTERN INDIA THERE WERE ENORMOUS VOLCANIC ERUPTIONS AT THE TIME THE DINOSAURS DIED

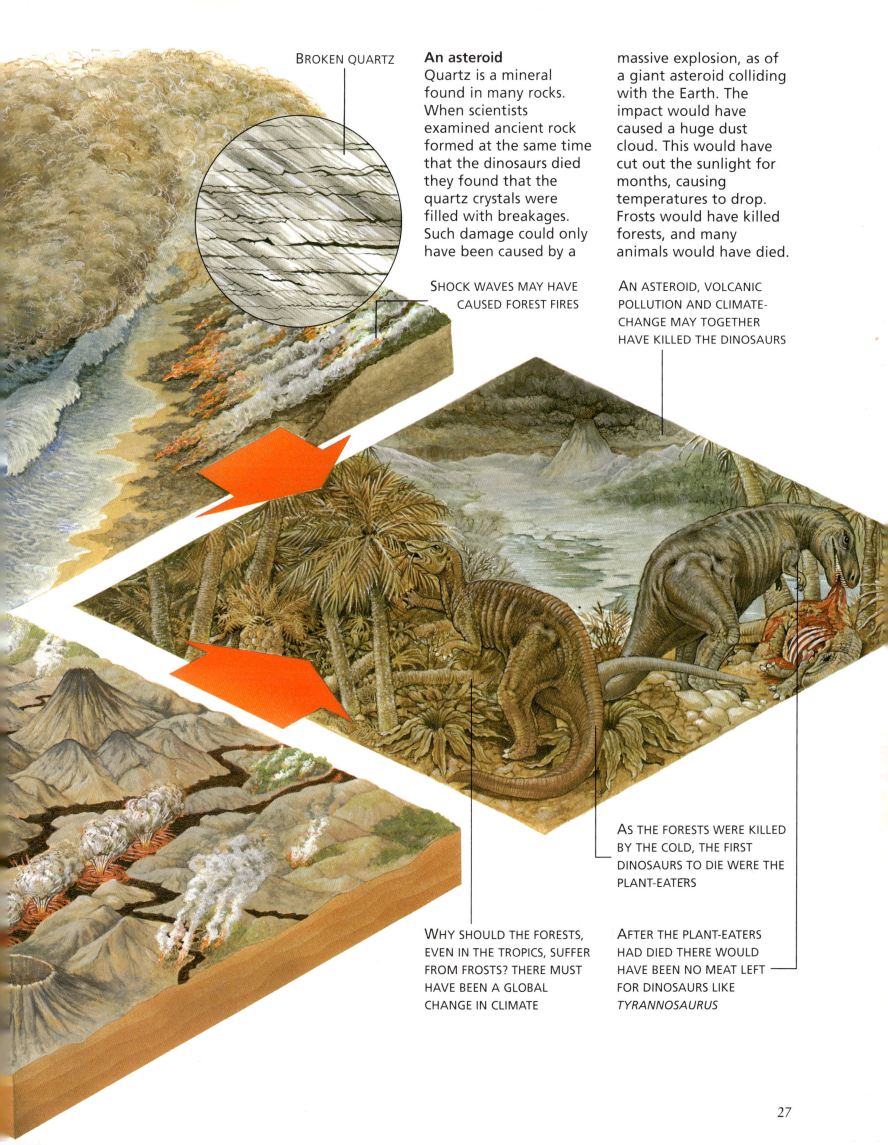

BROKEN QUARTZ

An asteroid
Quartz is a mineral found in many rocks. When scientists examined ancient rock formed at the same time that the dinosaurs died they found that the quartz crystals were filled with breakages. Such damage could only have been caused by a massive explosion, as of a giant asteroid colliding with the Earth. The impact would have caused a huge dust cloud. This would have cut out the sunlight for months, causing temperatures to drop. Frosts would have killed forests, and many animals would have died.

SHOCK WAVES MAY HAVE CAUSED FOREST FIRES

AN ASTEROID, VOLCANIC POLLUTION AND CLIMATE-CHANGE MAY TOGETHER HAVE KILLED THE DINOSAURS

AS THE FORESTS WERE KILLED BY THE COLD, THE FIRST DINOSAURS TO DIE WERE THE PLANT-EATERS

WHY SHOULD THE FORESTS, EVEN IN THE TROPICS, SUFFER FROM FROSTS? THERE MUST HAVE BEEN A GLOBAL CHANGE IN CLIMATE

AFTER THE PLANT-EATERS HAD DIED THERE WOULD HAVE BEEN NO MEAT LEFT FOR DINOSAURS LIKE *TYRANNOSAURUS*

Ancient Climates

CLIMATE is the weather observed over many years: how hot, cold, wet and dry it is. Climate affects the type of landscape, plants and animals that are found in a region. Over millions of years the climate of the world has changed. Sometimes there have been great ice-sheets over parts of the Earth. Sometimes deserts have covered whole continents, and then lush rain forest has grown on these same lands. Great forests have sunk to become barren salt lakes, and these in turn have been flooded as the rain returned. The continents have also moved across the globe, passing from one climate region to another.

When sediments are laid down they contain 'climate fossils' – evidence we can use to reconstruct the type of weather and landscapes that existed at that place millions of years ago.

DIFFERENT TYPES OF SEDIMENT ARE EVIDENCE OF DIFFERENT CLIMATES

REMEMBER: THE TOP SEDIMENTS ARE THE YOUNGEST; THE BOTTOM SEDIMENTS ARE THE OLDEST

LIMESTONE SEDIMENTS FORM IN SHALLOW SEAS

FOSSILS OF SEA-LIFE

DRY LAKES IN DESERTS LEAVE LAYERS OF SALTY SEDIMENT

FOSSILIZED RAIN FORESTS BECOME THICK LAYERS OF COAL (*SEE PAGES 30–31*)

TILTED SANDY LAYERS SHOW THERE WERE ONCE SAND DUNES

AS GLACIERS MELTED THEY LEFT THICK PILES OF MUD AND BOULDERS

ICE-AGE RIVERS DROPPED THICK SEDIMENTS IN THE SUMMER, BUT LITTLE IN THE WINTER, WHEN THEY FROZE

EVEN AFTER THE ICE MELTED, EVIDENCE OF THE ICE AGE WAS LEFT BEHIND

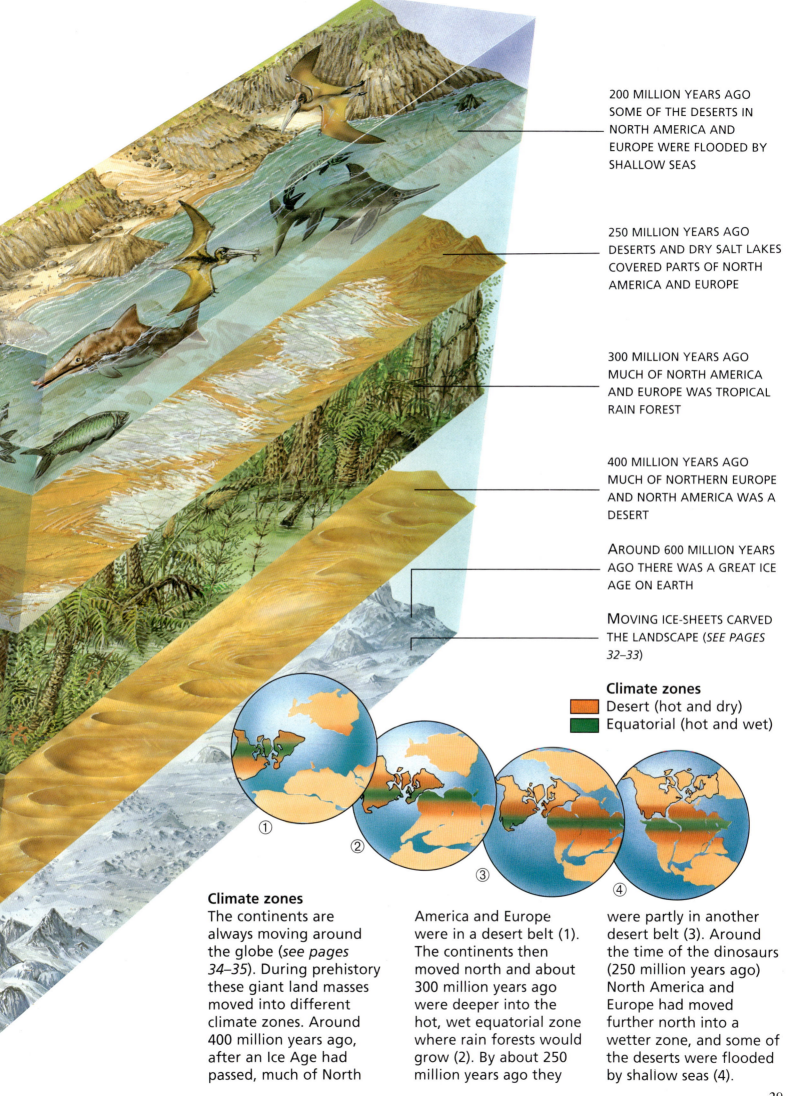

200 MILLION YEARS AGO SOME OF THE DESERTS IN NORTH AMERICA AND EUROPE WERE FLOODED BY SHALLOW SEAS

250 MILLION YEARS AGO DESERTS AND DRY SALT LAKES COVERED PARTS OF NORTH AMERICA AND EUROPE

300 MILLION YEARS AGO MUCH OF NORTH AMERICA AND EUROPE WAS TROPICAL RAIN FOREST

400 MILLION YEARS AGO MUCH OF NORTHERN EUROPE AND NORTH AMERICA WAS A DESERT

AROUND 600 MILLION YEARS AGO THERE WAS A GREAT ICE AGE ON EARTH

MOVING ICE-SHEETS CARVED THE LANDSCAPE (*SEE PAGES 32–33*)

Climate zones
🟧 Desert (hot and dry)
🟩 Equatorial (hot and wet)

① ② ③ ④

Climate zones

The continents are always moving around the globe (*see pages 34–35*). During prehistory these giant land masses moved into different climate zones. Around 400 million years ago, after an Ice Age had passed, much of North America and Europe were in a desert belt (1). The continents then moved north and about 300 million years ago were deeper into the hot, wet equatorial zone where rain forests would grow (2). By about 250 million years ago they were partly in another desert belt (3). Around the time of the dinosaurs (250 million years ago) North America and Europe had moved further north into a wetter zone, and some of the deserts were flooded by shallow seas (4).

Carboniferous Forests

THE FIRST primitive plants moved out of the water onto the land about 420 million years ago. The first tropical rain forests formed about 70 million years later, and in another 50 million years the forests covered enormous areas of lowland. In the forests the plants grew into giant, tree-like forms, reaching higher and higher above each other, seeking the sun. Below the tree-tops the crowded forests were dark and damp. These forests were much like today's rain forests, although many of the trees looked very different and there were no birds or monkeys. Instead, in the air and on the forest floor, there were giant insects. There were also large, fish-eating amphibians living in the swamps. We know what lived in these rain forests because a great many fossils were left behind in the rock we call coal.

GIANT CLUBMOSSES GREW IN THE SWAMPS

GIANT TREE FERNS

Evidence from coal
The first rain forests appeared in the Carboniferous period. When the trees in the early forests died they sank into a swamp (1). Here, where the land was slowly sinking, rotting leaves and logs gradually formed a damp soil called peat (2). As the layer of peat became covered by more sediment, the water in it was squeezed out. Over millions of years more and more water was squeezed out until it became coal. All that we know about the first rain forests has come from studying pieces of coal, the material that is dug from coal mines and burned in power stations (3).

A LAYER OF ROTTING PLANT AND ANIMAL REMAINS

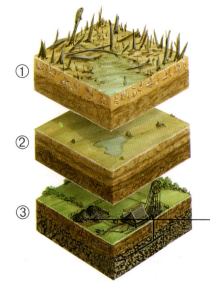

① ② ③

A LAYER OF PEAT, WHICH SLOWLY TURNED INTO COAL OVER MILLIONS OF YEARS

THE COAL THAT WE BURN IN FIRES IS THE REMAINS OF 300-MILLION-YEAR-OLD RAIN FORESTS!

GIANT MILLIPEDES, UP TO TWO METRES LONG, CRAWLED ACROSS THE FOREST FLOOR

GIANT DRAGONFLIES, WITH
WINGSPANS OF UP TO 70
CENTIMETRES, FLEW
THROUGH THE AIR

FOSSIL TREE-TRUNKS SHOW
THAT THE TREES REACHED
HEIGHTS OF 30 METRES

THIS GIANT CLUBMOSS IS
CALLED A *LYCOPTERIS*

Fossils from the forest
Coal comes from dead
plants. Well-preserved
fossils of leaves, stems
and trunks are often
found in coal, although
they are always highly
compressed (squashed).
The rings of this fossilized
tree-trunk have been
compressed.

The bark of the tree
lycopteris, a giant
clubmoss, had over-
lapping scales. Fern-
leaf fossils are often
found in coal.

Most of the insects alive
300 million years ago
would look familiar
today, although many
were much larger than
we would expect.

Fossils of the *Eryops*
show that it was the
largest of the early land-
living amphibians.

THE LARGE AMPHIBIAN
ERYOPS LIVED IN THE RAIN
FOREST – DINOSAURS HAD
YET TO APPEAR ON EARTH

EOGYRINUS WAS ANOTHER
FISH-EATING AMPHIBIAN – IT
LIVED IN THE SWAMP, LIKE
AN ALLIGATOR

THE JAW OF *ERYOPS* OPENED
DOWNWARDS, WHICH
WOULD HAVE BEEN IDEAL
FOR CATCHING FISH

Ice Age

THE plains of northern Europe and northern North America are filled with strange mounds and ridges. The soils contain stones and boulders, some of which have been carried there across hundreds of kilometres. The mountains of northern Europe and Canada are rounded and smoothed, as if worn down and polished by a sculptor. In the high mountains of California and the Alps, however, there are sharp mountain peaks, and in the mountain valleys there are lakes. All these features have been formed by moving ice. For a long period up until 12,000 years ago, these regions were covered by thick ice-sheets. By comparing land today with how it looked in the past, we can see how the ice-sheets changed the landscape.

AS THE GLACIER CARVED THE MOUNTAINS, IT LEFT SPIKY 'ALPINE' PEAKS

THE ICE FLOWED DOWNHILL LIKE A GREAT TONGUE OF STICKY LIQUID

THE LARGEST CONTINENTAL ICE-SHEETS MAY HAVE BEEN 3000 METRES THICK

UNDER THE HUGE WEIGHT OF MOVING ICE, THE LANDSCAPE WAS CARVED AND SCULPTED

THE GLACIER CARRIED SHARP BOULDERS IN THE ICE, WHICH SCRATCHED DEEP GROOVES IN ROCK SURFACES

ROCKS AND DEBRIS WERE DEPOSITED BY THE ICE-SHEETS, FORMING HILLS CALLED DRUMLINS

HUGE BOULDERS WERE CARRIED BY THE ICE AND DROPPED HUNDREDS OF KILOMETRES AWAY

Drumlins

Where the ice-sheets flowed over and around hard rocks, debris carried by the ice was dropped. The piles of debris rose higher and higher until rounded hills, called drumlins, were formed.

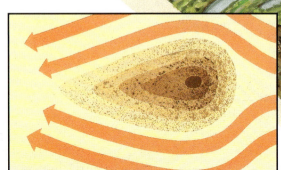

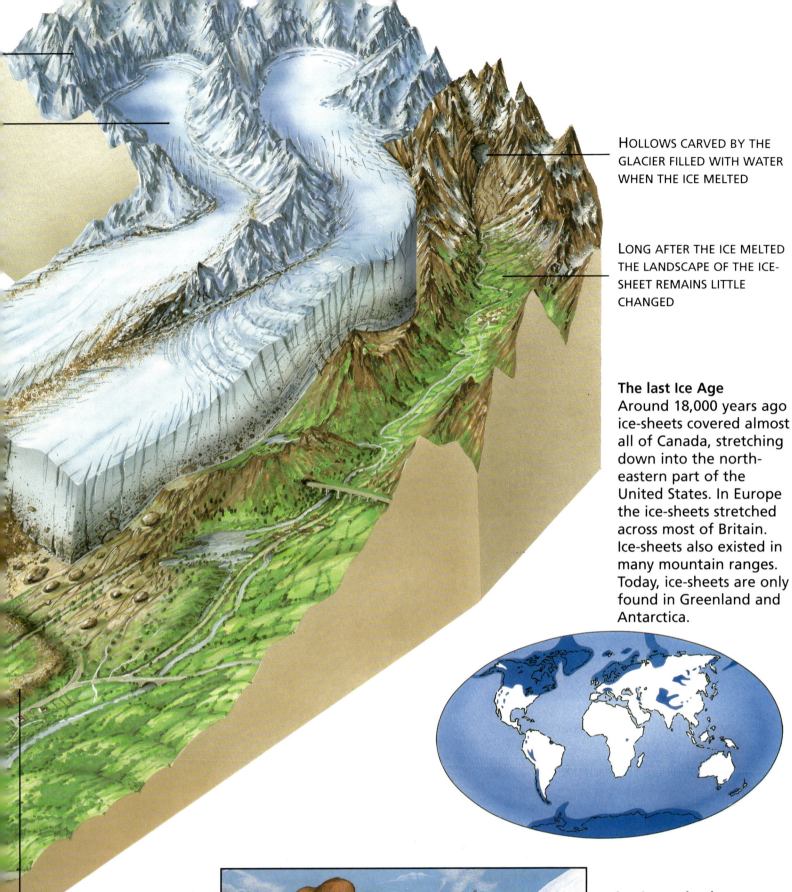

HOLLOWS CARVED BY THE GLACIER FILLED WITH WATER WHEN THE ICE MELTED

LONG AFTER THE ICE MELTED THE LANDSCAPE OF THE ICE-SHEET REMAINS LITTLE CHANGED

The last Ice Age

Around 18,000 years ago ice-sheets covered almost all of Canada, stretching down into the north-eastern part of the United States. In Europe the ice-sheets stretched across most of Britain. Ice-sheets also existed in many mountain ranges. Today, ice-sheets are only found in Greenland and Antarctica.

ALL OVER THE REGION ONCE COVERED BY THE ICE THERE ARE MORAINES: SANDY SOILS FILLED WITH STONES AND BOULDERS

ROADS OR RAILWAYS SOMETIMES FOLLOW ANCIENT MORAINE RIDGES

Ice Age animals

The animals that lived on the plains next to the ice-sheets included the mammoth, an extinct relative of the elephant, with a woolly coat. The tusks and bones of mammoths are sometimes found in marshland far away from the ice-sheets of today.

Drifting Continents

SINCE the Earth first formed, its continents have been moving across the globe. Volcanic eruptions and earthquakes are visible signs that the continents crash into and slide past one another. Yet the continents' movements are very slow – just a few centimetres each year. Rocks hold many clues as to the speed and direction of the continents' movements over the past hundreds of millions of years. They can tell us about the different climates the land has experienced, as the continents have moved towards or away from the equator (*see pages 28-29*). The best clues come from evidence of the Earth's magnetism that is trapped in rocks.

200 MILLION YEARS AGO TODAY'S CONTINENTS WERE JOINED INTO ONE SUPERCONTINENT, CALLED PANGAEA

ECHIDNA

GLOSSOPTERIS
PLATYPUS

Plants and animals
The fern *glossopteris* once grew widely on the supercontinent Pangaea. Fossils of the fern are now found in all the lands that made up the supercontinent. The primitive animals echidna and platypus live in Australia, but animals very like them live far away on the continent of South America. They drifted apart on the moving continents, having once lived on the same single supercontinent.

The Earth's magnetism
The Earth's magnetic field is generated by the movement of hot liquid metal in the centre of the Earth. The lines of magnetic force curl through the Earth, causing the needle of a compass to point north.

LINES OF MAGNETIC FORCE

NORTH

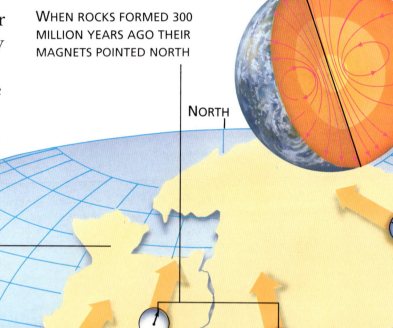

WHEN ROCKS FORMED 300 MILLION YEARS AGO THEIR MAGNETS POINTED NORTH

NORTH

SOUTH

THE GREEN AREA SHOWS WHERE *GLOSSOPTERIS* GREW ACROSS PANGAEA

AROUND 250 MILLION YEARS AGO PANGAEA STARTED TO BREAK APART

Magnets in rock

When the hot liquid rock that lies deep in the Earth seeps up onto the Earth's surface through a volcano, it cools and hardens. This causes its iron-rich crystals to solidify and become magnetized. These tiny magnets all point in the direction of the Earth's magnetic field – north. The magnets are all set, 'frozen' in time, pointing in the same direction. If the continents then move, carrying the rocks with them, the 'frozen' magnets may no longer point north. By measuring the direction in which the ancient rock magnets now point, it is possible to know where the rock was when it formed. By looking at many rock magnets, scientists can work out where an entire continent used to be.

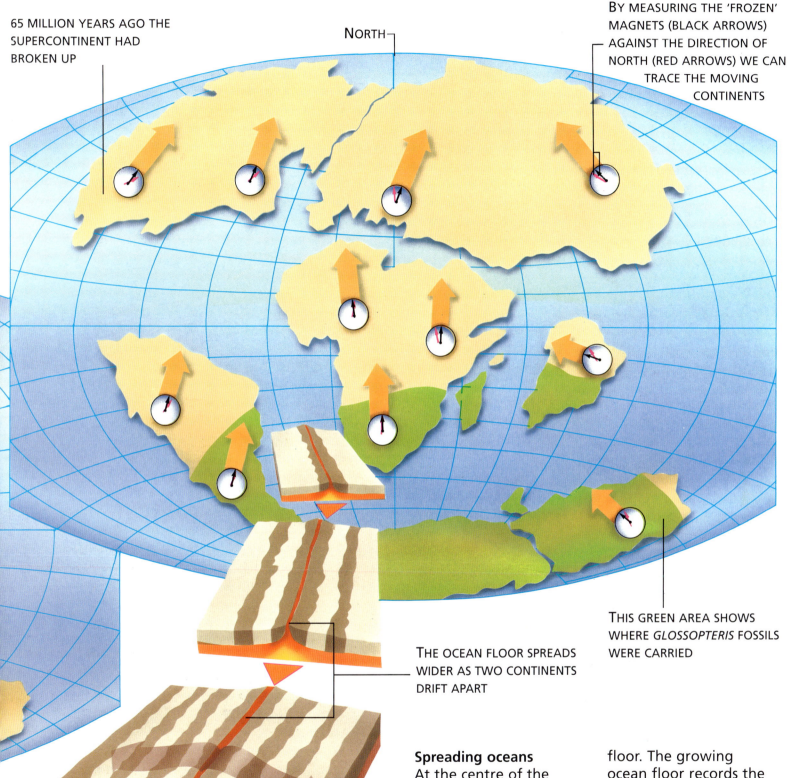

65 MILLION YEARS AGO THE SUPERCONTINENT HAD BROKEN UP

NORTH

BY MEASURING THE 'FROZEN' MAGNETS (BLACK ARROWS) AGAINST THE DIRECTION OF NORTH (RED ARROWS) WE CAN TRACE THE MOVING CONTINENTS

THIS GREEN AREA SHOWS WHERE *GLOSSOPTERIS* FOSSILS WERE CARRIED

THE OCEAN FLOOR SPREADS WIDER AS TWO CONTINENTS DRIFT APART

Spreading oceans

At the centre of the Atlantic Ocean floor lies a ridge where two continents are drifting apart. As they separate, hot liquid rock oozes out and solidifies to fill the gap left in the ocean floor. The growing ocean floor records the Earth's magnetic field. It shows that about twice every million years, the Earth's magnetic field switches direction, so compasses would point south, not north!

Changing Sea-levels

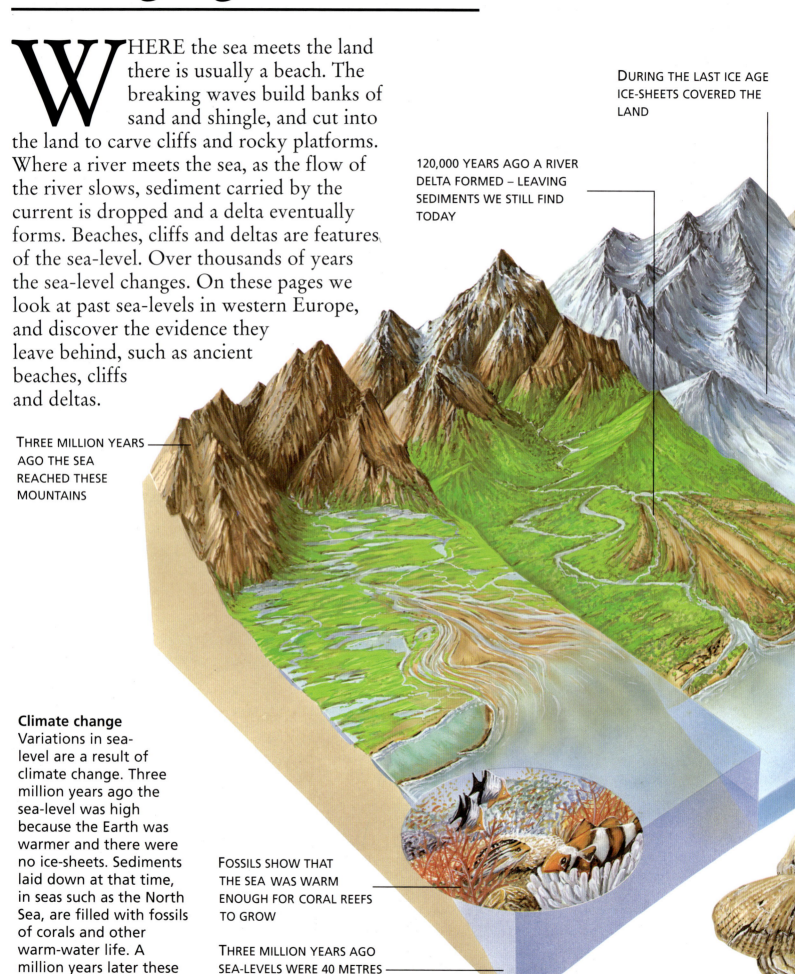

WHERE the sea meets the land there is usually a beach. The breaking waves build banks of sand and shingle, and cut into the land to carve cliffs and rocky platforms. Where a river meets the sea, as the flow of the river slows, sediment carried by the current is dropped and a delta eventually forms. Beaches, cliffs and deltas are features of the sea-level. Over thousands of years the sea-level changes. On these pages we look at past sea-levels in western Europe, and discover the evidence they leave behind, such as ancient beaches, cliffs and deltas.

THREE MILLION YEARS AGO THE SEA REACHED THESE MOUNTAINS

DURING THE LAST ICE AGE ICE-SHEETS COVERED THE LAND

120,000 YEARS AGO A RIVER DELTA FORMED – LEAVING SEDIMENTS WE STILL FIND TODAY

Climate change
Variations in sea-level are a result of climate change. Three million years ago the sea-level was high because the Earth was warmer and there were no ice-sheets. Sediments laid down at that time, in seas such as the North Sea, are filled with fossils of corals and other warm-water life. A million years later these seas were covered in ice!

FOSSILS SHOW THAT THE SEA WAS WARM ENOUGH FOR CORAL REEFS TO GROW

THREE MILLION YEARS AGO SEA-LEVELS WERE 40 METRES HIGHER THAN TODAY

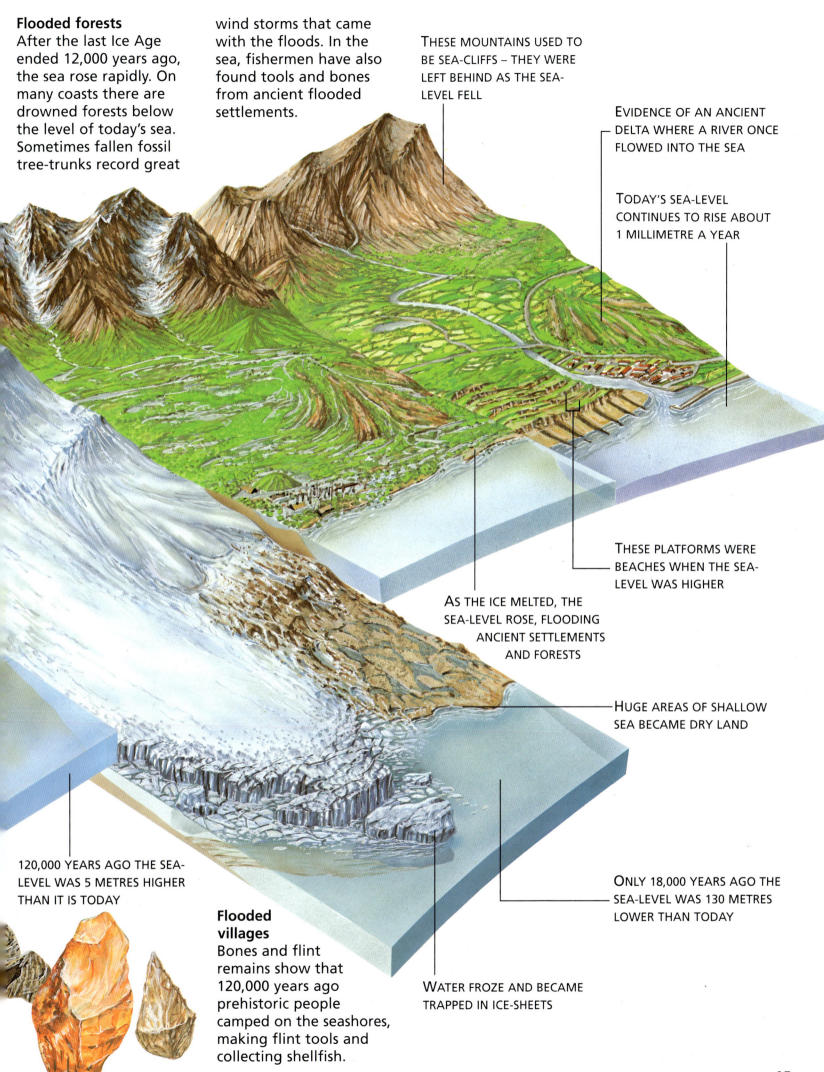

Flooded forests

After the last Ice Age ended 12,000 years ago, the sea rose rapidly. On many coasts there are drowned forests below the level of today's sea. Sometimes fallen fossil tree-trunks record great wind storms that came with the floods. In the sea, fishermen have also found tools and bones from ancient flooded settlements.

THESE MOUNTAINS USED TO BE SEA-CLIFFS – THEY WERE LEFT BEHIND AS THE SEA-LEVEL FELL

EVIDENCE OF AN ANCIENT DELTA WHERE A RIVER ONCE FLOWED INTO THE SEA

TODAY'S SEA-LEVEL CONTINUES TO RISE ABOUT 1 MILLIMETRE A YEAR

THESE PLATFORMS WERE BEACHES WHEN THE SEA-LEVEL WAS HIGHER

AS THE ICE MELTED, THE SEA-LEVEL ROSE, FLOODING ANCIENT SETTLEMENTS AND FORESTS

HUGE AREAS OF SHALLOW SEA BECAME DRY LAND

120,000 YEARS AGO THE SEA-LEVEL WAS 5 METRES HIGHER THAN IT IS TODAY

ONLY 18,000 YEARS AGO THE SEA-LEVEL WAS 130 METRES LOWER THAN TODAY

Flooded villages

Bones and flint remains show that 120,000 years ago prehistoric people camped on the seashores, making flint tools and collecting shellfish.

WATER FROZE AND BECAME TRAPPED IN ICE-SHEETS

Mountain Building

MOUNTAINS rise, are worn down, and eventually disappear. Across the world there are mountains at different stages of this cycle. The highest are formed where continents collide. The Himalayas, rising to more than eight kilometres, are forming where the Indian land mass is crashing into the rest of Asia. Some mountains are volcanoes, forming where molten rock, or magma, from deep in the Earth pours out at its surface. Others are made from deep-sea sediments that were deposited by rivers and have since been thrust high into the sky. While some mountains are rising, many are slowly being worn away. By studying rocks from mountains at these different stages, geologists are able to build a model of the life cycle of an ancient mountain range.

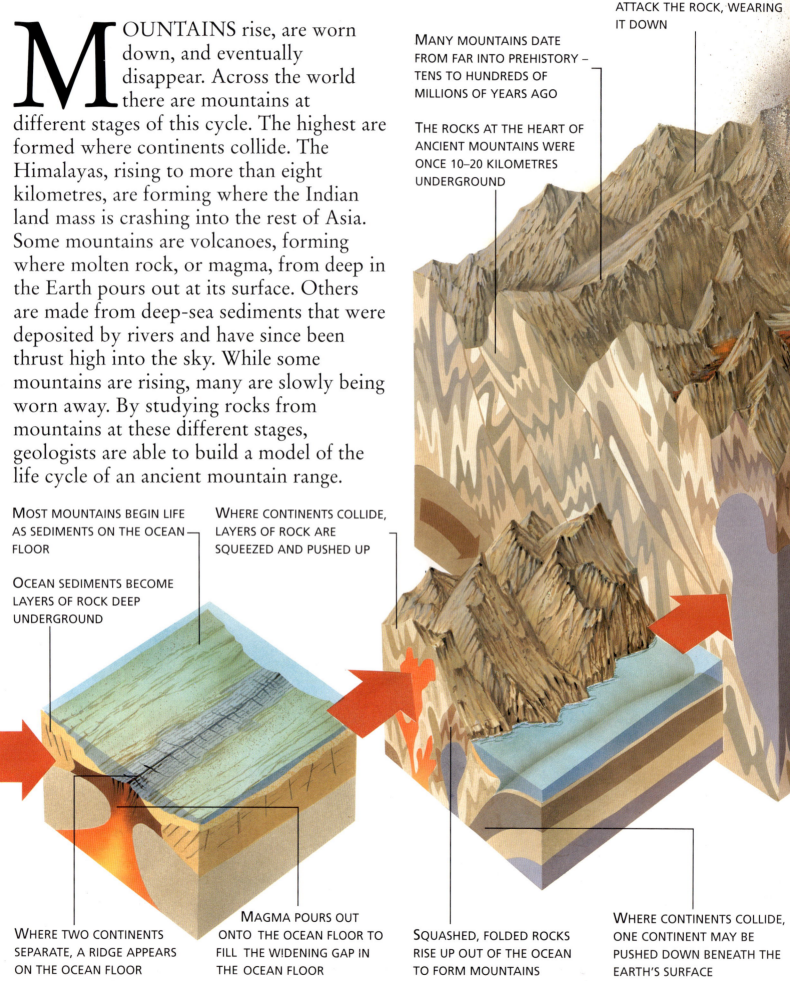

SNOW, ICE, WIND AND RAIN ATTACK THE ROCK, WEARING IT DOWN

MANY MOUNTAINS DATE FROM FAR INTO PREHISTORY – TENS TO HUNDREDS OF MILLIONS OF YEARS AGO

THE ROCKS AT THE HEART OF ANCIENT MOUNTAINS WERE ONCE 10–20 KILOMETRES UNDERGROUND

MOST MOUNTAINS BEGIN LIFE AS SEDIMENTS ON THE OCEAN FLOOR

OCEAN SEDIMENTS BECOME LAYERS OF ROCK DEEP UNDERGROUND

WHERE CONTINENTS COLLIDE, LAYERS OF ROCK ARE SQUEEZED AND PUSHED UP

WHERE TWO CONTINENTS SEPARATE, A RIDGE APPEARS ON THE OCEAN FLOOR

MAGMA POURS OUT ONTO THE OCEAN FLOOR TO FILL THE WIDENING GAP IN THE OCEAN FLOOR

SQUASHED, FOLDED ROCKS RISE UP OUT OF THE OCEAN TO FORM MOUNTAINS

WHERE CONTINENTS COLLIDE, ONE CONTINENT MAY BE PUSHED DOWN BENEATH THE EARTH'S SURFACE

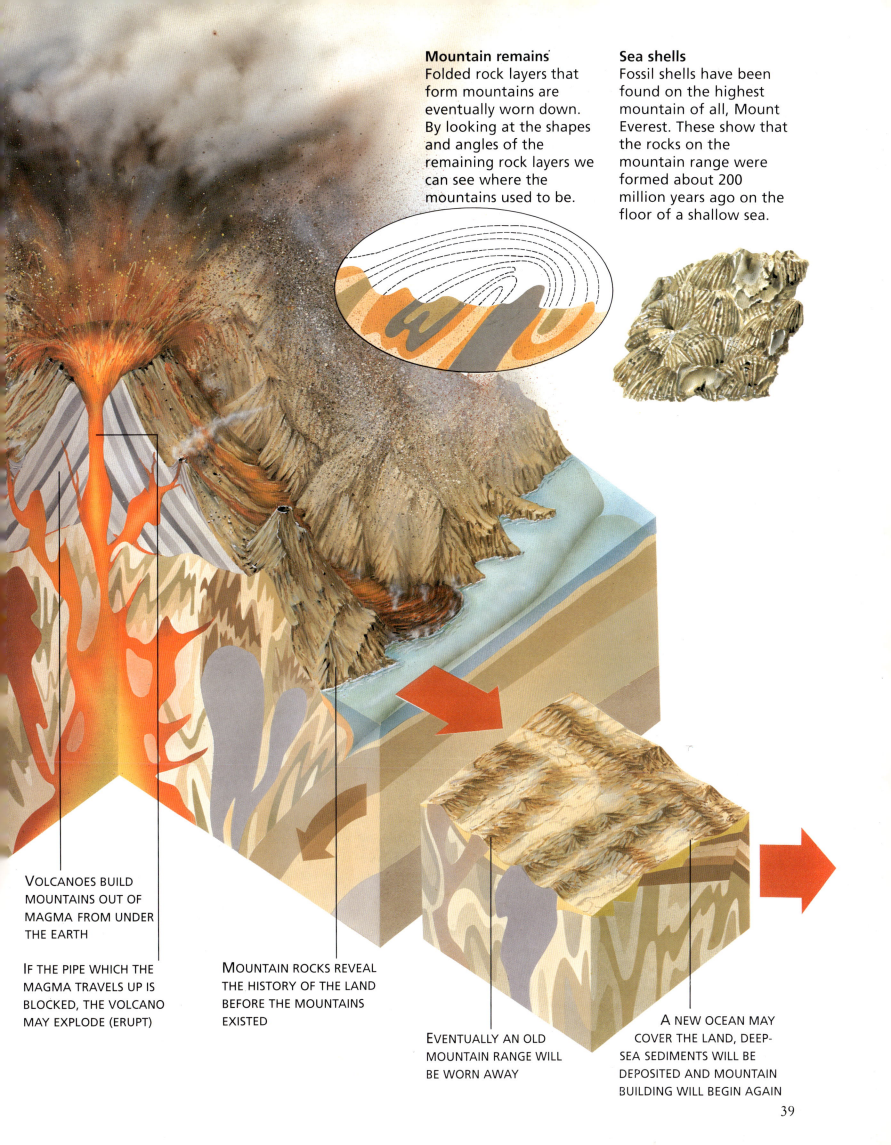

Mountain remains
Folded rock layers that form mountains are eventually worn down. By looking at the shapes and angles of the remaining rock layers we can see where the mountains used to be.

Sea shells
Fossil shells have been found on the highest mountain of all, Mount Everest. These show that the rocks on the mountain range were formed about 200 million years ago on the floor of a shallow sea.

VOLCANOES BUILD MOUNTAINS OUT OF MAGMA FROM UNDER THE EARTH

IF THE PIPE WHICH THE MAGMA TRAVELS UP IS BLOCKED, THE VOLCANO MAY EXPLODE (ERUPT)

MOUNTAIN ROCKS REVEAL THE HISTORY OF THE LAND BEFORE THE MOUNTAINS EXISTED

EVENTUALLY AN OLD MOUNTAIN RANGE WILL BE WORN AWAY

A NEW OCEAN MAY COVER THE LAND, DEEP-SEA SEDIMENTS WILL BE DEPOSITED AND MOUNTAIN BUILDING WILL BEGIN AGAIN

Early Peoples

A T THE same time that northern Europe was covered in ice-sheets, there were forests in the river valleys of south-western France. Beneath soils of wind-driven dust and river sediment, archaeologists have found traces of the people who lived in this region between 15,000 and 10,000 BC. These Magdalenian people were hunters, living on the large herds of animals that moved through the valleys. Food was plentiful and the people had time to create new tools and even make ornamental objects. The Magdalenian people have left many clues as to how they lived. By excavating the region, we have been able to build up a picture of their lives.

Wall paintings
The people of this region painted pictures of the animals they hunted, such as this bison, along the walls of caves. Forms of natural mineral dye, such as red ochre, were used as paint.

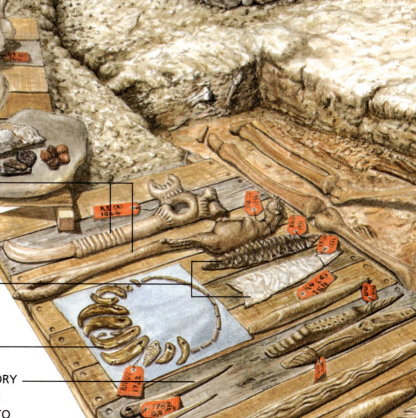

THE HEARTH OF A FIRE LEAVES A PATCH OF BURNT BONES, SCORCHED STONES AND CHARCOAL FRAGMENTS

EXCAVATED REMAINS HAVE BEEN ASSEMBLED ON BOARDS AND LABELLED

MAMMOTH AND ANTLER BONE WERE CARVED INTO TOOLS

FLINT ARROWS AND SPEAR-HEADS WERE FITTED ONTO WOODEN STICKS, WHICH HAVE SINCE ROTTED AWAY

PIECES OF A SHELL AND BEAR-TOOTH NECKLACE HAVE BEEN FOUND AND GATHERED TOGETHER

NEEDLES MADE FROM IVORY (MAMMOTH TUSKS) WERE USED FOR SEWING SKINS TO MAKE CLOTHES

BONES REVEAL THE RANGE OF ANIMALS THAT WERE EATEN

STONES AROUND A SAUCER-SHAPED HOLE MARK THE SITE OF A TENT-LIKE HOME

THIS BISON WAS CARVED OUT OF A REINDEER ANTLER

THIS SITTING BEAR WAS CARVED OUT OF SOFT STONE

THIS HUNTER WAS BURIED IN A SPECIAL CEREMONY, SURROUNDED BY WEAPONS AND TOOLS

RADIOCARBON DATING OF THE BONES SHOWS THAT THIS MAN AND THE ANIMALS ARE FROM THE SAME PERIOD

Clues to a lifestyle

Fossils from the site of the Magdalenian people show they hunted herds of bison and reindeer, and also fished. Their food was cooked over a fire. They probably lived in communities and exchanged goods with other members of their tribe. From their carvings we can tell that they communicated with other tribes across the whole of central Europe. Objects found at their burial places seem to show they believed the dead would live again in this, or another, world. The Magdalenians were among the first humans to make art objects. Items such as carved animals may have been more than ornaments, having magical importance.

Skins for warmth

The Magdalenian people lived only a few hundred kilometres south of the ice-sheet, so it was not very warm. Animal skins were used for clothing, as well as for lining their tent-like homes.

Reconstructing Faces

WHAT were the first human beings like? The only remains that archaeologists have found are fragments of fossil bones and skulls. Bones of early humans known as *Australopithecus Afarensis* have been found in sediments laid down in eastern Africa. We can tell the age of these bones from the volcanic ash sediments in which they are found. The sediment layers were dated using the potassium-argon radio-isotope technique (*see pages 16–17*), and found to be more than three million years old. Fossils of the legs of a female *Australopithecus* show that these ancient humans walked upright. Fully grown, a female was around 150 centimetres tall.

After piecing together fragments of the skull we can also tell what the face of this prehistoric human looked like. On these pages we see the processes involved in reconstructing the face.

1) The clay model

Fossil skulls are rarely complete. Fragile bones such as those of the nose tend to splinter and are lost. So the first job is to repair the skull. Pieces are glued together and missing sections filled with plaster.

By looking at the skull, and at the muscles on faces of modern human beings, scientists can work out where the muscles would have been. The face muscles are formed on the skull using clay. Careful measurements of the skull are also taken to decide how big the nose and eyes should be.

For the skin on the *Australopithecus,* a simple layer of clay, 2–3 millimetres deep, is added. This final layer is shaped and sculpted with wrinkles and lines to make it more realistic.

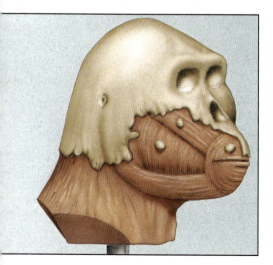

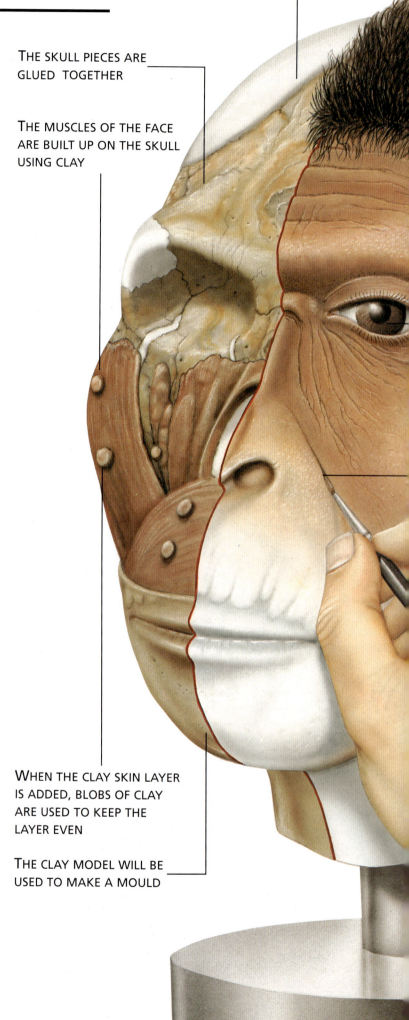

MISSING PARTS OF THE FOSSIL ARE FILLED WITH PLASTER

THE SKULL PIECES ARE GLUED TOGETHER

THE MUSCLES OF THE FACE ARE BUILT UP ON THE SKULL USING CLAY

WHEN THE CLAY SKIN LAYER IS ADDED, BLOBS OF CLAY ARE USED TO KEEP THE LAYER EVEN

THE CLAY MODEL WILL BE USED TO MAKE A MOULD

2) The plastic copy

When the clay model is complete, rubber is poured over it to make a mould. When the mould is ready, plastic is poured into it and left to set. The rubber mould is then peeled off leaving a rigid plastic copy of the clay model. The clay model, containing the precious bone, can be returned to the museum. The plastic copy is passed over to the artist.

EARS, LIKE THE NOSE, HAVE TO BE SCULPTED INTO SHAPES BASED ON APES' AND HUMAN EARS

GLASS EYES OF THE CORRECT SIZE ARE INSERTED INTO THE EYE SOCKETS

THE SKIN IS RECREATED IN A COLOUR TYPICAL OF THIS HOT REGION OF AFRICA

THE HARD PLASTIC MODEL IS PAINTED

A LASER BEAM SCANS THE SKULL

HUMAN HAIR IS USED TO MAKE SURE IT LOOKS REALISTIC

3) The completed face

The model is brought to life with paint, glass eyes and hair. The amount of hair on the *Autralopithecus* can only be guessed at, although the hair on modern humans and living apes can be used as a guide. The amount of hair added changes the appearance greatly.

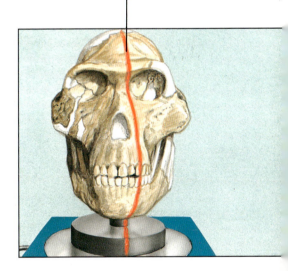

Computer faces

Computers are also used to reconstruct faces. The skull is scanned by a laser so that its exact shape can be seen on a computer screen. Muscles and skin are added onto the image electronically. Different skin tones and hair length or colour can be tested, too

Early Beliefs

MUCH of what we know about prehistoric peoples comes from the many monuments they left behind. Some of these were built as burial chambers; others were used for ceremonial purposes. Among the most mysterious monuments is Stonehenge: 162 blocks of stone, built on a plateau in southern England. Most of our discoveries about the monument and the people who built it have come from excavations at the site. We know that some of the stones were quarried hundreds of kilometres away, and that it probably took hundreds of men to haul just one of them. The immense effort involved suggests the people had very strong reasons for building Stonehenge.

Why was Stonehenge built?

The sun aligns with certain stones at the mid-summer and mid-winter solstice (the longest and shortest days of the year). The sun also aligns with stones at the equinoxes (days of equal day and night). So it is possible that Stonehenge was used as an astronomical calendar, showing when to plant crops or observe festivals.

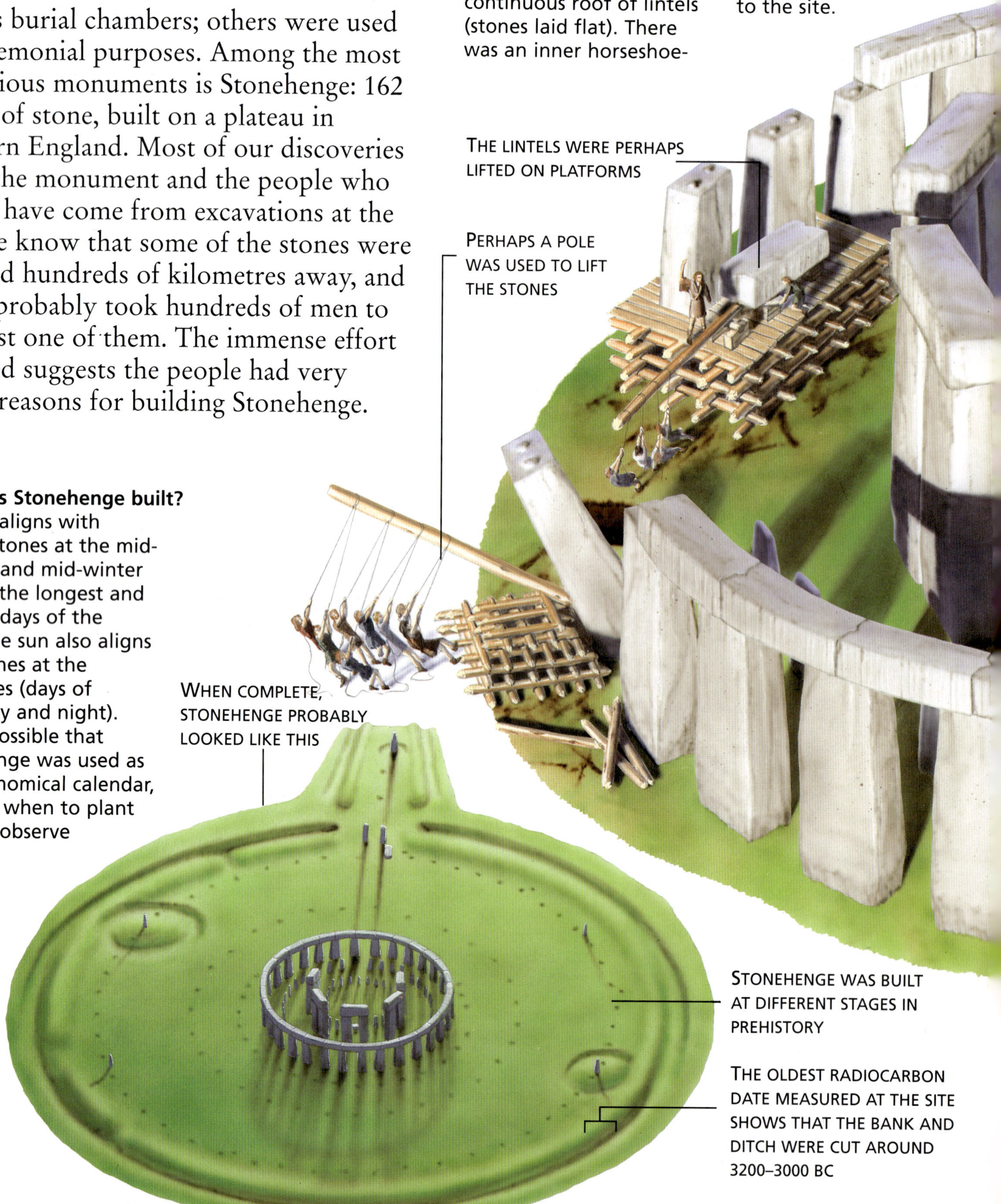

Stonehenge

The picture below shows three stages in the life of Stonehenge: its building (*below*), its completion (*centre*) and the ruins left today (*right*).When complete, Stonehenge comprised a ring of upright stones with a continuous roof of lintels (stones laid flat). There was an inner horseshoe-shaped ring of five pairs of separate uprights, each pair with its own curved lintel. Inside both rings stood smaller stones (bluestones). The monument was in the middle of a round bank surrounded by a ditch, and a broad avenue led to the site.

THE LINTELS WERE PERHAPS LIFTED ON PLATFORMS

PERHAPS A POLE WAS USED TO LIFT THE STONES

WHEN COMPLETE, STONEHENGE PROBABLY LOOKED LIKE THIS

STONEHENGE WAS BUILT AT DIFFERENT STAGES IN PREHISTORY

THE OLDEST RADIOCARBON DATE MEASURED AT THE SITE SHOWS THAT THE BANK AND DITCH WERE CUT AROUND 3200–3000 BC

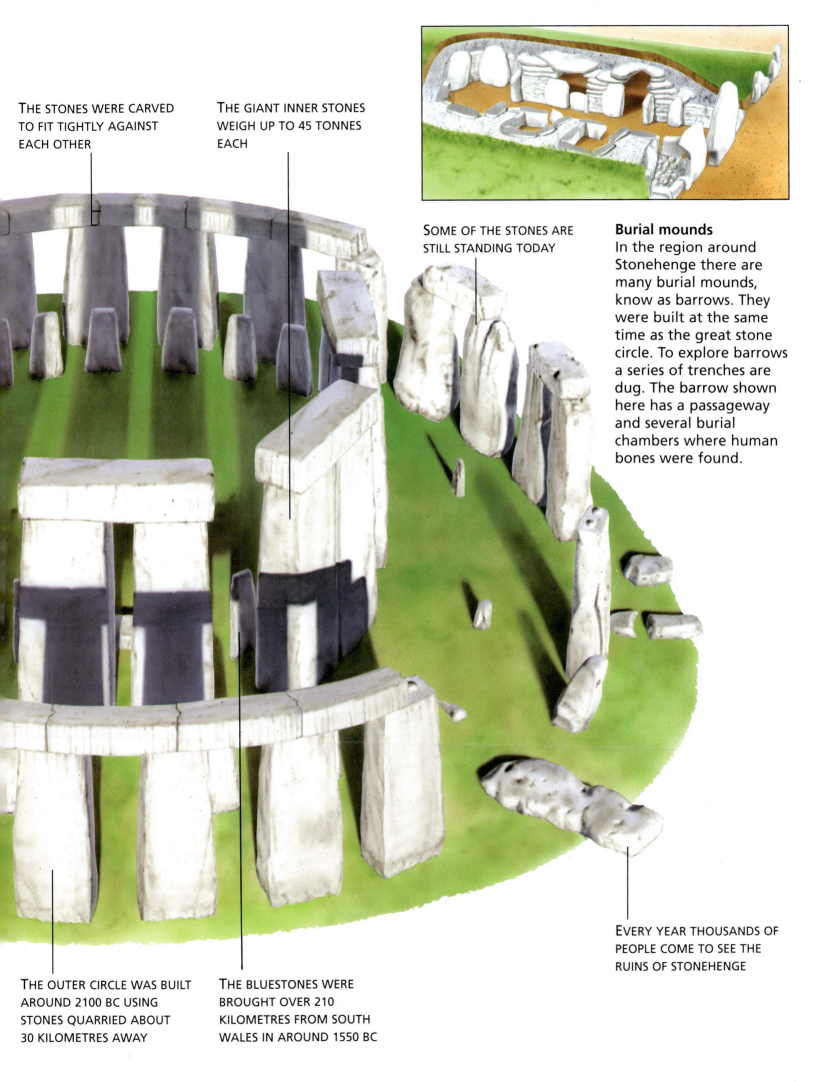

THE STONES WERE CARVED TO FIT TIGHTLY AGAINST EACH OTHER

THE GIANT INNER STONES WEIGH UP TO 45 TONNES EACH

SOME OF THE STONES ARE STILL STANDING TODAY

Burial mounds

In the region around Stonehenge there are many burial mounds, know as barrows. They were built at the same time as the great stone circle. To explore barrows a series of trenches are dug. The barrow shown here has a passageway and several burial chambers where human bones were found.

THE OUTER CIRCLE WAS BUILT AROUND 2100 BC USING STONES QUARRIED ABOUT 30 KILOMETRES AWAY

THE BLUESTONES WERE BROUGHT OVER 210 KILOMETRES FROM SOUTH WALES IN AROUND 1550 BC

EVERY YEAR THOUSANDS OF PEOPLE COME TO SEE THE RUINS OF STONEHENGE

Index